66245

THE ENGLISH NOVELISTS
General Editor:
HERBERT VAN THAL

RONALD FIRBANK

RONALD FIRBANK

by

JOCELYN BROOKE

LONDON
ARTHUR BARKER LTD.

First published 1951

Printed in Great Britain by
THE CAMPFIELD PRESS ST. ALBANS
FOR ARTHUR BARKER LTD., 3C MUSEUM STREET, LONDON, W.C.1

CONTENTS

TO

BRYHER

WITH GRATITUDE

AUTHOR'S NOTE

All students of Firbank must be heavily indebted to Mr. Ifan Kyrle Fletcher's *Ronald Firbank: A Memoir*, published by Messrs. Gerald Duckworth in 1930. I am no exception; and would like here to express my gratitude to Mr. Kyrle Fletcher and to Messrs. Duckworth for permission to quote biographical and other details from this indispensable work.

My thanks are due also to Messrs. Gerald Duckworth and to Col. Thomas Firbank for permission to quote from the works of Firbank himself. I should like also to express my gratitude to the following for their kind assistance: Miss Nina Hamnett, Mrs. Eileen Bigland, the late Lord Berners, Sir Osbert Sitwell, Mr. Harold Nicolson, Mr. Mervyn Horder, Mr. Desmond MacCarthy, Mr. Jonathan Curling, Mr. Augustus John.   J. B.

INTRODUCTION

(I)

"TO break a butterfly, or even a beetle, upon a wheel," writes Mr. E. M. Forster, in his admirable essay on Ronald Firbank,[1] " is a delicate task." Mr. Forster's warning is very much to the point, and should be pondered by all who feel impelled to write about Firbank; for, to attempt any " serious estimate " of him, to try to " assess his importance," and so on, is indeed to break the most delicate and elusive of butterflies upon the clumsiest of wheels; or, to vary the metaphor (for Firbank, to my mind, suggests botanical rather than entomological parallels) it is as though one should press some rare orchis between blotting-paper. A shapeless brown blob is the result: duly classified and labelled no doubt, but, were it not for the label, entirely unrecognizable.

Why then write about him at all? A critical biography of Firbank—the idea is a quenching one; Firbank, one feels, must be turning (or at least wriggling) in his grave at the mere suggestion of such an enormity. For one may as well say it right away: you either like Firbank or you don't, and no amount of criticism, however sympathetic, will ever create a taste for him in those who find him uncongenial. The only excuse for writing a book about him is, I think, that he has, in recent years, been largely neglected; his novels have been allowed to go out of print,[2] and a whole

---

[1] *Abinger Harvest.*

[2] Since this was written, five Firbank novels have been reprinted in an " omnibus " edition by Messrs. Duckworth (1949).

generation has grown up, since his death, which has barely
heard of him. He is overdue for resurrection; and if one is
debarred, out of respect for his memory, from saddling him
with some ponderous " Life," he can at least, I think, be
" presented " for the benefit of those who have never read
him. He cannot, like Messrs. Walpole and Galsworthy, be
neatly pigeon-holed in the dreary files of " Eng. Lit.";
the most one can do is to disinter him, like some elusive
orchid, from the jungle of half-forgotten " fiction," and
restore him to the light of day. Such, at any rate, is the sole
aim of the present study; and if a subterranean wriggle
disturbs momentarily the soil of that Roman cemetery where
he lies buried, one can only hope that Ronald will not (in
his own words) be " more than perhaps just a little shocked "
at the impertinence. At least, one feels, he will not object
to the orchidaceous simile; for did he not himself bestow
upon an (alas! fictitious) orchid the honour of his own name
—" Ronald Firbank, a dingy lilac blossom of rarity untold "?[1]

(II)

" . . . Oh, those Tales—those Tales! How shall I describe them?
Fabulous characters shoot across his pages like gaily dressed
performers on the trapeze. . . . The verbal surface of his writing
is rich and fantastically diversified. The wit is incessant. . . . . "

Thus Mr. Scogan, in Aldous Huxley's *Crome Yellow*,
eulogizes the great Knockespotch—whose wondrous " Tales,"
alas! exist merely as part of a row of dummy books in
Mr. Wimbush's library. " It was Knockespotch," Mr.
Scogan adds, " who delivered us from the dreary tyranny
of the realistic novel. . . . I am tired " (he said) " of seeing

[1]See *Prancing Nigger*.

the human mind bogged in a social plenum; I prefer to paint it in a vacuum, freely and sportively bombinating."

Knockespotch, one feels, might almost have written *Valmouth* or *The Flower beneath the Foot;* and one wonders whether Mr. Huxley, when he conceived this *éloge*, had Firbank in mind. Mr. Arthur Waley, in his Introduction to Firbank's Collected Works, writes in a somewhat similar strain, hailing Firbank as a rebel against naturalism at a time when the English novel was "still in the Chantrey Bequest stage."

This, I think, is somewhat to overstate the case: Firbank was never, at any rate consciously, a revolutionary—rather the reverse, in fact. Essentially a man of the nineties, born a couple of decades too late, he harked back, with perpetual nostalgia, to the *époque mauve*. His earliest story (*Odette d'Antrevernes*) is a feeble pastiche of the worst, most senti-mental kind of Yellow Booksiness; in his later work he "reacts" not, I think, against any literary school, but merely against himself—he has learnt to laugh at his own extreme *fin-de-sièclisme*. None the less, the ninetyish influence is never forgotten, and recurs again and again in the later novels—usually in the guise of parody or conscious pastiche, but sometimes, as we shall see, quite seriously and without disguise.

There is, in fact, a curious ambivalence in his work, a perpetual conflict between his ninetyish sensibility and a cynical self-mockery which somewhat recalls the similar case of his contemporary, Philip Heseltine. In Heseltine the two modes existed separately: "Peter Warlock" bears little or no relation to the composer of *The Curlew*. In Firbank, they co-existed: in his best work the conflict is resolved; and it is, I think, this resolution of two conflicting tendencies which gives his writing its unique quality.

Mr. Waley compares his prose with impressionist painting, but a more fruitful comparison, surely, would be with *musical* impressionism: one might say of Firbank's prose, as it used to be said of Debussy's music, that it has " no tune." Instead of being constructed on a basis of continuous " melodic " development, it is built up from a number of short, detached phrases, woven together to form a complex musical pattern. (We know that this was, in fact, precisely Firbank's method of working: he would note down isolated phrases and sentences on scraps of paper, and hoard them for future use; often—for he was a careless worker in some respects—he would inadvertently use them twice over.)

The musical analogy can perhaps be extended; for, if Firbank's prose has no " tune," it is based, none the less, on a kind of counterpoint, in which the two tendencies— sentimental and self-mocking—are all the time apparent: sometimes diverging, sometimes mingling, often—for this " counterpoint " is, so to speak, atonal—producing, by their sudden interlocking, effects as strange and unpredictable as the dissonances of Schönberg or of Webern.

Firbank, indeed, though frivolous by intention and possessing the authentic " light touch," cannot be called an " easy " writer in the " twopenny library " sense. The average novel-addict, coming upon *Valmouth* for the first time, is likely to be discouraged by the over-elaborate sentences, the ninetyish affectations, the perpetual " showing-off." For Firbank is a master of pastiche—his style, indeed, is really a kind of exuberant " dressing-up," and suggests the pranks of a highly-sophisticated child let loose in the old-clothes chest. The chest is ransacked for bustles, kilts, corsets, crinolines— anything will come in handy, the more unsuitable or incongruous the better. One feels, too, that this " dressing-up " is essentially a semi-private affair—its chief object is to amuse Firbank himself, or at most a drawing-room audience composed of a few chosen friends. His work, indeed, displays throughout an aristocratic disdain for the common reader: Firbank will make no concessions, the conventions of the ordinary novel are thrown overboard, those of us who are not " in the know " must sink or swim.

The peculiar, rather disjointed construction of most of the novels has, I think, a very simple explanation: Firbank simply left out the parts which he found boring to write. The framework, the " scaffolding " which supports the structure of the conventional novel, is dispensed with; the discursive explanations, the descriptive *longueurs* are ruthlessly deleted. The alert reader usually tends to " skip " such passages in any case; in Firbank's novels the " skipping " is done, so to speak, in advance, by the author himself. In consequence his stories have an economy, a closeness of texture which amounts to a kind of novelistic shorthand.

If one had to classify Firbank (which God forbid) under one or other of the various sub-categories of " The Novel," one would, I suppose, have to call him a fantasist. But I should not, myself, be quite happy about the classification. Fantastic he certainly is, but the term " fantasy," applied to his novels, implies an element of whimsy which I think is misleading. He could be whimsical, but whimsy is never an integral part of his technique.

Mr. Waley has compared Firbank to a butterfly, hovering always an inch or two above the surface of things; but there is, as Mr. Forster points out, something of the beetle about him too—a kind of flying beetle, perhaps, who may hover, but is incapable of any lengthy or sustained flight. There is something, in fact, incorrigibly *terre-à-terre* about Firbank, which

distinguishes him from the true fantasists. Consider, for
instance, his use of the supernatural; he introduces it, in
passing, as it were, and one accepts it as nothing out of the
way—as in the case of the nun in *Cardinal Pirelli*, " who was
inclined to give herself married airs, since she had been
debauched, one otiose noon, by a demon." The nun is not
an important character—she does not reappear, nor does the
demon; a moment later we are brought safely back to earth,
the stream of diffuse, mannered dialogue is resumed, and the
demon is forgotten. It is " fantasy " of a kind, I suppose;
but not, by any means, the kind which usually goes by that
name.

(III)

Firbank, I suppose, is thought of chiefly as a " humorous "
writer, and humorous he certainly is; but his humour is of a
very special order. His characters and situations may be and
often are extremely funny in themselves; but Firbank's
particular brand of humour is typically of the purely *verbal*
kind, depending on the very shape and cadence of the
sentence. I have used the word " humour " with intention,
in preference to " wit ": for wit implies the epigrammatic,
and, in spite of Firbank's debt to the nineties, there are almost
no epigrams, in the ordinary sense of the word, to be found
in his work. (His attempts at the genuine Oscar-ish article, as
in his early sketch, *A Study in Temperament*, are best forgotten.)

Firbank's humour lies in the inflection, the tone of voice;
his dialogue teems with innuendo, a whole character is
implied in a phrase; the dying fall of a cadence, the displaced
adverb provoke a sudden giggle: Firbank will write, for
instance, " he groomed fitfully his hair," or " Will you not
make, Andrew, that appalling noise? "—inversions which
give to his prose a kind of syncopated quality which suggests

jazz-music—an effect which, indeed, was probably intentional. Typical, too, is the following sentence, with its note of elaborate pastiche (which seems an echo from Ouida):

> "'I so feared he was going to be shy!' With pensive psychic fingers the enamoured Englishwoman toyed with a talismanic bagatelle in New Zealand jade . . ." (*Valmouth*).

Sometimes the wit spills over into a sort of nonsense-poetry, recalling Edward Lear:

> "Here and there, upon the incomparably soft grey hills, a light shone like a very clear star.
> "'How admirable' . . .
> "'Though to my idea,' Lady Georgia said, 'the hills would undoubtedly gain if some sorrowful creature could be induced to take to them. I often long for a bent, slim figure, to trail slowly along the ridge, at sundown, in an agony of regret' . . ." (*Vainglory*).

Firbank's mannerisms can be irritating—alliteration, for instance, is a habit of his, and though more often than not he uses it with economy and tact, he sometimes overdoes it:

> "The plaintive pizzicato of Madame Mimosa's Pom pup 'Plumbun' . . ." etc. (*Valmouth*).

Note, too, the artfully-artless cadence of this sentence:

> ". . . 'And afterwards, just to break the ice, I intend to take you to an Oriental restaurant in Soho' . . ." (*Inclinations*).

Such tricks as these would be exasperating in some writers; but with Firbank they are an integral part of his style, and indeed (for in Firbank's case, if ever, the style was the man) of himself.

It would be a thankless task to sort out Firbank's "influences" from a style so overloaded with conscious and mischievous borrowings. He is fond, for instance, of parodying the gossip-column (*The Flower beneath the Foot*), but one can hardly say that he is "influenced" by *The Tatler* —any more than one can accuse Picasso of being "influenced" by *Le Journal* or *Paris Soir* because he chooses to stick cuttings from these papers across some of his pictures. Firbank's most obvious debt is, of course, to the nineties—more especially to Maeterlinck and the French symbolists. (Among English works of the period which most evidently influenced him, one can single out, I think, Beardsley's *Venus and Tannhaüser*.) Other sources include Restoration plays and French eighteenth-century memoirs; and it seems to me obvious, too, that Firbank was an addict of late-Victorian lady-novelists such as Ouida and Marie Corelli. In the case of Ouida, indeed, though he delights to parody her, one cannot help suspecting that Firbank took her more than half seriously (and indeed, Ouida is a much underrated novelist).[1] Certain scenes in Ouida immediately suggest Firbank: for example, the first chapter of *Friendship*, in which the two austere Scottish dames visit their erring relative in Rome. While on the subject of influences, it may be worth noting, too, the occasional similarities between Firbank and " Baron Corvo " —though this is rather, perhaps, a case of two largely dissimilar writers borrowing from the same sources.

Firbank's admiration for Maeterlinck, so evident in his early work, was never, one suspects, more than half serious. (As early as 1905, in *A Study in Temperament*, he could be satirical at Maeterlinck's expense.) Certainly, the Maeterlinckian influence was soon displaced by others. Firbank was, after all, very much an *enfant de son siècle*, and took a lively interest in contemporary movements: one can assume that his reaction against Maeterlinck and the nineties generally was hastened considerably by his reading of Apollinaire, Cocteau and their associates. At a slightly later date he

[1] I am indebted to my friend Miss Nina Hamnett for pointing out to me Ouida's influence upon Firbank.

doubtless appreciated, also, the earliest Eliot (*Prufrock*) and the Edith Sitwell of the *Façade* poems. (*Prufrock*, indeed, with its blend of ninetyish sensibility and "post-war" cynicism is closely akin to Firbank.)

Firbank was not, as I have already remarked, a conscious revolutionary; but, as Mr. Cyril Connolly has pointed out, he was "a true innovator, and his air of ephemerality is treacherous in the extreme."[1] His innovations were unobtrusive: he was not, by nature, the kind of writer who becomes an "influence," a *chef d'école*. It is the task of every artist, as Mr. Forster has said somewhere, to extend, by however little, the area of human perception and sensibility. Firbank did, undoubtedly, help to push the enveloping darkness a little further back; but he happened to be pushing at a point where too many had pushed before him, and which, perhaps, was always more resistant than most. In his own *genre*, he could go no further himself, and the path he took is closed to his successors: there have been attempts to imitate him, but these have been quickly and deservedly forgotten. His influence is perceptible, perhaps, in the early novels of Aldous Huxley and in those of Evelyn Waugh; but it was never more than a faint echo, and, as the work of Messrs. Waugh and Huxley has become progressively more "serious," so the echo has diminished.

(IV)

Mr. W. H. Auden once confessed[2] that the writers whom he would most have wished to "write like" were "Firbank, Potter, Carroll, Lear." Three of these, it may be noted, are writers of books for children. Firbank, certainly, is very far

[1] *The Condemned Playground.*
[2] *Letters from Iceland.* (*Letter to Lord Byron.*)

from being a children's writer; but he has certain points in common with the other three, and one of these, I think, is the quality of innocence.

It is a surprising statement to make about Firbank—he is, after all, an extremely sophisticated writer, and often very indecorous. What one really means by his " innocence " is the complete absence from his work of any moral judgment. Perhaps this is one reason why Firbank has never been widely popular—for no Englishman feels quite happy about a work of art which has not some sort of moral purpose;[1] and so far as I know, no literary laboratory test has yet been devised that will detect the least trace of any moral purpose in Ronald Firbank. (He may occasionally introduce a " moral " element, as in *Prancing Nigger*, but one feels that its function in such cases is purely æsthetic.) One can't even, in Firbank, detect any specifically *immoral* purpose, as one can, perhaps, in Beardsley. Firbank, in fact, was nearer than almost any other English writer to being a pure artist. This is not to say, of course, that he was always a *good* artist: he was, as a matter of fact, a very unequal writer, and could be irritatingly bad at times (even his spelling and grammar were well below matriculation standards); but he did genuinely practise the doctrine of *art pour l'art*, and I can think of hardly any other English prose-writer, except perhaps Joyce, who did this—though many have tried to, especially, of course, Wilde (who, however, was a moralist *malgré lui*).

Mention of Beardsley recalls the fact that Firbank has been described as a " Beardsley in prose." It is not a very good comparison; it does not sum up Firbank by any means; but it provides a clue. For Firbank has this much in common with

---

[1] Oddly (or perhaps not so oddly?) Firbank has always been more popular in America than in his own country.

Beardsley—he created a uniquely personal world of his own. A page of Firbank is as unmistakable as a Beardsley drawing; and it is, I think, this ability to create a self-contained universe, unlike any other, that made Auden bracket Firbank with Edward Lear and Beatrix Potter.

This " world " of Firbank is congenial or not, according to one's temperament. Firbank's personality shines through his books like that of no other writer, and it is not the sort of personality that everybody can put up with. *Valmouth* and *Cardinal Pirelli* will never, one feels, be very popular with Low-Churchmen or with the sterner type of Rugger-hearty; nor, indeed (let us hasten to add), was Firbank himself, in his lifetime. " It would be impossible, I feel, to actually be as decadent as Lambert looked," wrote Mr. Harold Nicolson in a semi-fictitious study which embodies more than a little of Firbank himself.[1] But Firbank, in real life, was quite as decadent as he looked, if not more so. Certainly he *looked* decadent—we have ample evidence on this point; and in his tastes, his habits, his complex and tremulous temperament he was the very apotheosis of what is politely called " æstheticism "; one might say, indeed, that in him the *fin-de-siècle* achieved, belatedly, its full and final flowering.

By the time Firbank came to maturity, æstheticism was already unfashionable: the Wilde trials had dealt it a blow from which it was never to recover, and after 1900 " decadence " was admissible, among the English upper-class, only as a " phase " of adolescence. Undergraduates were expected (unless they were out-and-out hearties) to pass through a " decadent " period; but the young man who remained impenitently a decadent after taking his Schools had become a rarity. Aestheticism in its extreme form was

[1] *Some People.*

considered (perhaps not unfairly) a mark of the second-rate;
and as a (so to say) post-graduate æsthete it was a foregone
conclusion that nobody should take Firbank seriously. Even
by his best friends Ronald was never, in his early days,
considered much more than " promising "; and to say of a
young man, ten years after he has left the university, that he
is promising, is usually a polite way of calling him a failure.

Firbank, it may be added, was not merely the apotheosis of
æstheticism; he was also its *reductio ad absurdum*. There is a
story, quoted by Mr. Ifan Kyrle Fletcher,[1] which shows just
how irritatingly ninetyish he could be on occasion. He had
been dining with some friends at a restaurant (probably the
Tour Eiffel in Percy Street) and was already driving away in a
taxi when one of his companions called after him: " Good-
night, Firbank." The taxi immediately pulled up, and its
occupant craned his head out of the window. " I wish," he
called back, in shrill and agonized tones, " I *wish* you wouldn't
call me ' Firbank '—it gives me a sense of goloshes."

Yet Firbank, after all, was to give the lie to his critics.
Damned in his early days as " promising," he contrived
brilliantly, none the less, to fulfil his promise. A parallel case
springs to mind—that of another *dilettante*, Marcel Proust, the
spoiled darling of the Faubourg St. Germain, always too
much occupied, first by the *monde*, afterwards by illness, to
begin his *magnum opus*; who, nevertheless, to the astonishment
of all who knew him, lived to write what is probably the
greatest (and certainly the longest) novel of the century.

Firbank's triumph was on a smaller scale: he didn't write
a *magnum opus*—nor, indeed, did he ever cherish so tedious an
ambition. He did, however, forge for himself a style which
was the perfect expression of his fantastical, hypersensitive

[1] *Memoir.*

and rather unhappy temperament; and though handicapped, like Proust, by chronic ill-health and by an insatiable taste for society, contrived to write a series of novels in which a few people will always find a perennial delight. His works will never, certainly, be an obligatory subject for " Eng. Lit."; nor, thank goodness, will they ever be " popular." *Valmouth* and *Vainglory* will remain, merely, for some people their favourite bedside books—people, for the most part, who remember the *Tour Eiffel* and the old Café Royal, the *Trois Colonnes* in the Rue de Lappe and the " Welcome " at Villefranche. A younger generation, it may be hoped, will also read and enjoy him: they will not remember his background, or the places and the people from which (however tenuously) his " world " derives; but they will find in his books, perhaps, an echo of that life, and will be able to enjoy, at however distant a remove, some of the transitory, forgotten gaieties of a world remote, now, as Babylon or Knossos.

CHAPTER I

THE LIFE AND THE LEGEND

(I)

FIRBANK became a legend in his own lifetime—a legend which, for that matter, he did all in his power to foster; so much so, that it is difficult for his biographer to disentangle the reality from the self-engendered myth. I doubt, indeed, whether such a task is possible: for Firbank, unlike many artists, was very much of a piece; his legend is hardly more fantastic than his historic personality, and his books are a mere extension of himself. One could say, indeed, almost with equal truth, that he himself is a mere extension of his books: certainly he wanders in and out of them with a perfectly natural air—as Claud Harvester in *Vainglory*, as himself (off-stage) in *The Flower beneath the Foot*, as an orchid in *Prancing Nigger*. And, from contemporary accounts, one would scarcely have been surprised, it seems, if one had called upon him in Rome or in Piccadilly, to find him in the company of Mr. Winsome Brookes or of Lady Parvula de Panzoust.

The legend survived his death—with such vitality, indeed, that it was firmly believed in some quarters, for a considerable time afterwards, that he was not dead at all. His death, people said, was just another of his fantastic inventions: in reality he was sitting comfortably in Haiti or Kamschatka giggling with malicious delight over his own obituaries.

Arthur Annesley Ronald Firbank was born in London in

1886, the second son of Sir Thomas Firbank, and grandson of Joseph Firbank, an immensely successful railway contractor. Ronald's heredity disproves a deeply-rooted popular belief, i.e. that the typical " æsthete," hypersensitive, neurotic and often sexually abnormal, is (like des Esseintes) invariably the end-product of an inbred and degenerate line of ancestors. Joseph Firbank, Ronald's grandfather, was the son of an illiterate Durham miner, and himself began his career in the pits at the age of seven. He happened to be a genius—though of a very different kind from his grandson. His life was one of the typical " success stories " of the Victorian commercial world, a chapter out of Samuel Smiles. He attended night-classes, and at the age of twenty-one, obtained a job as a labourer on a local railway then under construction. Here his genius blossomed; trains, it was evident, were to be his destiny. His cleverness and efficiency were rewarded by quick promotion; bigger and better opportunities presented themselves, and were snapped up by young Joseph with avidity and an unerring foresight. He never looked back: by 1866 he was one of the largest contractors in the country.

He remained to the last a typical " Geordie " in his manners and his accent; he died in 1886 (the year of his grandson's birth) in the odour of Victorian-Liberal-commercial sanctity, immensely respected by all who knew him. He appears to have been a sympathetic character, popular not only with his big-business colleagues, but also with his employees, to whom he is said to have behaved generously. His eldest son, Sir Thomas, was a less remarkable personality: as Mr. Kyrle Fletcher[1] remarks, " the step from autocracy to pomposity is small." Joseph Firbank never became a " gentleman "; his son, naturally enough, grew up into the *haute bourgeoisie*,

[1] *Memoir.*

marrying the daughter of an Irish clergyman, and becoming in due course a Member of Parliament. His wife seems to have been sensitive and cultivated, and Sir Thomas, doubtless with her encouragement, became a well-known collector of prints and porcelain.

Into this tame, conventional and rather pompous *milieu* was born the author of *Valmouth* and *Cardinal Pirelli*. Not more incongruous, surely, was the birth of Marigold, the mulattress heir-presumptive of Hare-Hatch house (in *Valmouth*). In Firbank's birth as in his death, the fantastical note is characteristically in evidence:

> " *Ah! que n'ai-je mis bas tout un noeud de vipères,*
> *Plutôt que de nourrir cette dérision!* "

Thus might Firbank's parents, one feels, echoing Baudelaire, have greeted so strange a nativity.

Ronald was a delicate child, and suffered from an affection of the throat, for which reason he was often taken abroad; these early travels, besides benefiting his health, gave him a valuable advantage over most embryo-artists, enabling him to realize the existence (apart from " geography ") of other countries besides his own. In Firbank's case the lesson was certainly not wasted; and doubtless his childhood journeys sowed the seeds of that wanderlust which was to possess him throughout his life. He could never, in after years, settle down in England for long at a time: the English way of life was fundamentally alien to him; he craved for the sun, and like many an artist before him seemed naturally drawn to those European cities in which the Latin civilization most elegantly survives. At the same time he kept his roots in England (or at least in London); the *monde* fascinated him; he never became, like many of his contemporaries, permanently an expatriate. Nor did he develop that nagging hatred of England which afflicts, sooner or later, so many men of his particular temperament.

It would be out of place, in a study such as this, to deduce his mature personality, on Freudian lines, from his early upbringing. It is fairly obvious, however, that he was a classical, a positively " text-book " case of the " spoilt child," entirely dominated by his mother, to whom he was devoted. It is equally evident that he never managed, as most children do, sooner or later, to extricate himself from his " mother-fixation." He was delicate, his parents were rich and perhaps over-indulgent; from his earliest days his every whim was gratified; not surprisingly, he grew up to expect of the world at large a similar indulgence. Most young men would have suffered a rude awakening: but the world can prove surprisingly kind if only one has enough money, and Firbank, fortunately for himself (and perhaps for posterity) was rich enough to preserve his illusions almost intact.

There was, however, one short interlude in his early life during which he must have caught a glimpse (and perhaps more than a glimpse) of another kind of life. In 1900, when he was fourteen, he was sent to school for the first time: to Uppingham. One wonders what decided his family suddenly to plunge this sensitive, sickly child into the Moloch-jaws of a notoriously " hearty " public school; one suspects that Sir Thomas must, for the first (and probably the last) time, have put his foot down. Ronald had been too much indulged; it would do him good to live the life of a healthy, normal boy —thus, no doubt, argued his father, as most upper-class fathers are wont to argue. Possibly, also, there was another reason: Sir Thomas's own father, after all, had started life in the pit, and to nobody are the advantages of a public-school education so apparent as to the newly-enriched. However this may be, to Uppingham Ronald went: straight from a home life more than usually sheltered and luxurious, and without the normal prelude of a preparatory school, by which, in ordinary cases, the sensitive child is at least partly immunised against the worse horrors to come.

Ronald stayed two terms at Uppingham; it is somewhat surprising that he survived there so long. History is silent as to the details of his brief career at the school; but one may assume that a boy of his type suffered more acutely than most from the casual brutalities and injustices of public-school life. The commonly held theory is (or was in those days) that a public school is a testing-ground for character: the system was designed to " knock the nonsense out of " those who had the misfortune to possess " nonsensical " proclivities. Fortunately for us, Uppingham failed conspicuously during those two terms to knock any of Ronald's nonsense out of him. Had the process continued he might indeed have survived (for he possessed considerable adaptability of a kind); but he would not, at the end of four years, have emerged as the Ronald Firbank we know. The effect of such a schooling on one of his temperament is usually to turn out a dolt or a don—and more often than not (in the latter case) not a very good don. Firbank, fortunately, was reserved for a better fate.

Henceforward he was educated, as the phrase goes, " privately," by a tutor at Buxton. The normal rhythm of his life was resumed: home comforts, the indulgence of all his whims, trips abroad for his health.

The years passed happily: Ronald, one presumes, gave little thought to the future, though he may already, perhaps, have begun to dream of the books which he would one day write. These early projects, one imagines, bore little (if any) relation to *Prancing Nigger* or to *Valmouth*: probably he contemplated some tenuous, esoteric romance, or a verse-play such as Dowson's *The Pierrot of the Minute*. . . . But if Ronald took no thought for the future, Sir Thomas presumably did; one may indeed suppose that he was exceedingly puzzled by the problem of his son's career. For Ronald, obviously (as the son of his father), must have a career of some kind; if he did not, he would merely drift—and one knew where that led to. Several professions were ruled out: the Army, for instance. . . . Perhaps the Law? Or why not the Church? But no, not even the Church seemed quite the thing for Ronald. . . . Suddenly the solution presented itself—the only possible one: Ronald should enter the Diplomatic Service!

(II)

As Mr. Kyrle Fletcher[1] remarks, with gentle malice, " the Diplomatic Service was never embarrassed by the strangeness of his talents." The project, however, was set under weigh, and Ronald was sent, in 1904, to Tours, for the purpose of learning French. During his sojourn there, he not only learnt French, but discovered (which was more important) French literature. Here, too, no doubt, he acquired that taste for mediævalism (and particularly for the French middle-ages) which never left him. He may also, at Tours, have felt (as Mr. Kyrle Fletcher suggests) his first attraction toward the Roman Church; though this, in fact, would be a natural enough accompaniment to his growing ninetyishness. His early story, *Odette*, is set in the Loire country; but it might, for that matter, have been set anywhere else—the *mise-en-scène* is not very important. It is said that, in later life, Firbank would often talk about his time at Tours—but only to laugh

[1] *Memoir.*

at some odd episode which happened there. It does not seem likely (as has been suggested) that Firbank ever passed through any very serious mystical phase, at Tours or anywhere else; though no doubt he liked to play with the idea, just as " Eddie Monteith " (in *The Flower beneath the Foot*) harboured a passing ambition to become a Jesuit.

Still, no doubt, with the idea of studying for the Diplomatic Service, Ronald went in 1905 to Madrid, where he stayed for two months. Even more, perhaps, than his period at Tours, this Spanish journey was a formative experience: his love for Spain remained with him till the end of his days, and was fitly celebrated in the last of his novels, *Cardinal Pirelli*:

> " Spain! The most glorious country in God's universe, His admitted masterpiece, His gem. . . . "

Firbank was now nineteen; the delicate, retiring schoolboy, haunted by the shadow of those two terms at Uppingham, had blossomed into a fashionable, over-sophisticated young man. At Madrid he became a figure in local society; there are several extant accounts of him at this time: he is described by one of his Spanish friends,[1] " *alto, rubio, delgado y un poco presumtuoso, aunque con chic, un tanto afectadillo.*" He established himself in rooms in the Calle Mayor, where he lived surrounded by all those properties which were henceforward to form his background in whatever part of the world he might happen to find himself. . . . The chairs were draped with red silk; the fumes of incense hung thickly on the air; there were modern pictures, rare editions of contemporary authors, and always masses of flowers, usually out of season. . . . Here Firbank entertained his friends: feeling, for the first time, perhaps, that he was really a " personality," himself and no other. The chrysalis stage was over: the horrors of

[1] Antonio de Hoyos y Vinent, quoted by Ifan Kyrle Fletcher (*Memoir*).

Uppingham and the *nouveau-riche* pomposity of his family background were alike forgotten: the butterfly had emerged.

Returning from Spain to England, he entered the establishment of Mr. Scoones, lodging with Mr. de V. Payen-Payne, one of the tutors. The time had come to think about a university, and the choice fell, rather oddly, upon Cambridge. Surely, one feels, Firbank, if anybody, was destined, by his temperament, for Oxford; æstheticism, if not quite a lost cause, was decidedly losing ground, and might certainly be expected to survive more tenaciously in the home of lost causes, where the elder men still spoke of Pater and of Wilde. Perhaps, however, it was for this very reason that Sir Thomas preferred the idea of Cambridge: one sees in his choice a final attempt to wean Ronald from debilitating influences.

Lady Firbank, however, continued to spoil Ronald outrageously. When he arrived at the house of Mr. Payen-Payne he was accompanied by a footman and a housemaid, who entirely rearranged the new boarder's apartment in accordance with his mother's ideas of comfort. A new bed was provided, a special armchair, a luxurious eiderdown.[1] . . .

In October, 1906, Firbank went up to Trinity Hall, Cambridge. Not less curious than the choice of university was the choice of college. Trinity Hall, like Uppingham, had a reputation for extreme "heartiness," and one can hardly imagine a more unsuitable background for Ronald, " *delgado y un poco presumtuoso, aunque con chic,*" with his eiderdowns, his impressionist pictures, his incense and his flowers.

Oddly enough he seems to have escaped persecution at the hands of the hearties, though by all accounts he certainly asked for it. There is a story, related by Mr. Vyvyan Holland,[2] that Firbank was seen one day attired in shorts and

[1] *Memoir.*   [2] Ibid.

sweater, apparently returning from the football field. When asked whether this was indeed the case he replied in the affirmative: yes, he had been playing football. Rugger or soccer? Ronald wasn't sure. Was the ball round or oval? " Oh," exclaimed Ronald, " I was never *near* enough to it to see *that!* "

Before his arrival at Cambridge, Firbank had already published *Odette d'Antrevernes*, a fact which much impressed his fellow-undergraduates. To have published a real book when one was only nineteen! Firbank doubtless enjoyed his reputation as an established author, and as a special favour would present copies of *Odette* to his friends. Mr. Holland, who was editing the college magazine at the time, records that Firbank submitted at his request a contribution, which, however, was rejected on the grounds of its oddity. Already, it seems, Firbank had abandoned the style of *Odette*, and had begun to experiment in another manner; one wonders if the rejected " phantasy " of which Mr. Holland speaks, was perhaps a fragment from some early draft of *Vainglory* or *The Artificial Princess*.

If Firbank was indifferent to the sporting interests of his college, he was equally bored by the prospect of work. In fact he sat for no examinations—not even Littlego—and it is some tribute to the tolerance of the university authorities that Firbank was enabled to remain *in statu pupillari* for as long as he did. He went down in June, 1909, having completed only five of the usual nine terms; and, of course, without a degree.

(III)

The development of Firbank's personality was foreordained and inevitable; his life disproves all the theories about heredity and environment, and one cannot believe that he would have been very different, whatever the circumstances of his upbringing and subsequent career. Had his parents been poorer, had he been forced to adopt a definite profession, his talent might have been inhibited, he might—and indeed almost certainly would—have suffered agonies of frustration; but he would never, one can be sure, have settled down to the subfusc mediocrity of the professional man.

By the time he arrived at Cambridge Firbank was already a mature personality; his five terms at Trinity Hall brought him new contacts, he was continuously making fresh æsthetic discoveries, his religious leanings took a more definite shape: but the university was in no sense a crucial phase in his career, as it is in the lives of most young men. His time there was a pleasant interlude, nothing more; Cambridge became, for a while, one of his backgrounds: he was neither more nor less at home there than in London, Paris or Madrid.

Much of his time, during the vacations, must have been spent in Paris, for it is recorded that his Cambridge friends were much diverted by his anecdotes of Colette, Polaire, Pierre Louÿs and other Parisian acquaintances, as well as by his up-to-the-minute news of the latest in French painting and literature. At Cambridge he became a member of the Footlights Club, and frequented the Fitzwilliam Museum; but he seems to have taken little active part in the life of the university. His own life was centred in his rooms, which were furnished, like his lodgings in Madrid, with red silk draperies, masses of flowers, and innumerable books, pictures and statuettes—mostly, one suspects, of a character which must have seemed outlandish if not positively scandalous in the Cambridge of 1906. . . . In such surroundings he would entertain his numerous guests: not only his fellow undergraduates, but more distinguished friends from London and

Paris. His parties became famous: they were conducted with an elegance and luxury which the hearties of Trinity Hall doubtless wondered at and perhaps deplored. . . .

Among Firbank's closer friends at Cambridge were Vyvyan Holland, A. C. Landsberg and Rupert Brooke. The latter, at this time, was passing through the inevitable "decadent" phase—evident enough in the 1911 volume of poems—and he and Firbank were much preoccupied by the problem of evil. For Brooke the phase was a brief one, soon to be forgotten in the heroic excitements of 1914; Firbank, whose interest was deeper and more lasting, perceived that a belief in evil implies belief of another kind: it was but a step from *Les Fleurs du Mal* to the Church of Rome.

Firbank, indeed, had always possessed (like Lady Parvula de Panzoust in *Valmouth*) "latent proclivities." At Cambridge it was noticed that he was much in the company of Monsignor Barnes, then Catholic Chaplain to the University; and it occasioned little surprise among his friends when, in 1908, he was finally received into the Church.

His conversion seems to have had little if any noticeable effect on his customary way of life. He was, however, extremely reticent about such things, and it is impossible to say how much of his Catholicism was founded on true piety and how much on a merely æsthetic predilection. One cannot help suspecting that, like so many young men of *fin-de-siècle* sensibility, Firbank found in the Church a suitable "background" for his personality. On leaving Cambridge, he even considered the possibility of taking a post at the Vatican, in preparation for which he spoke of going into retreat: " as much for my looks as for the welfare of my soul." The Vatican, like the Diplomatic Service, was spared the embarrassment of Firbank's services; it appears, indeed, that the Church, in one way or another, failed to reciprocate his own enthusiasm, for in after years his Catholicism became purely nominal: " The Church of Rome wouldn't have me, and so I mock at her," he declared at a later date to Lord Berners.[1]

The true nature of Firbank's religious convictions must remain a mystery; but it is a fact that he was always extremely superstitious, and became more so in his later years. He could never resist fortune-tellers, however patently bogus, and toward the end of his life was on more than one occasion badly frightened by their gloomy prognostications. Linked with this vein of superstition was his admiration for Egypt and everything Egyptian: he was the possessor of innumerable amulets and statuettes, to which he paid a half-joking, half-serious homage. This taste is often manifested in his novels: Eddie Monteith, in *The Flower beneath the Foot*, is compared to a statue of Rameses, Mrs. Shamefoot (*Vainglory*) is accompanied everywhere by " a magnificent image of the god Ptah," and Mrs. Asp is writing " a life of Hepshepset, wife and sister of Thothmes II, who, on becoming a widow, invented a hairwash and dressed as a man."

Firbank's expressed intention to make a retreat " for the sake of his looks " cannot be regarded as wholly frivolous, for he was deeply enamoured of his own appearance, and had a genuine horror of losing his youthful charms. He would, even at this early date, diet himself drastically, and his incongruous début as a footballer was perhaps occasioned less by *esprit de corps* than by a desire to preserve the elegance of his profile. In later years his terror of growing stout became an obsession, and at dinner-parties he would refuse to eat more than a single peach (or, on one occasion, as

[1]*Memoir.*

C

Sir Osbert Sitwell records, a single green pea)[1]; it is almost certain that such a diet helped to undermine his always delicate health, and finally to hasten his death.

It is a curious fact that the numerous extant portraits of Firbank bear almost no resemblance to each other, seeming indeed, to depict a series of entirely disparate persons. During his life he was drawn or painted by Charles Shannon, Augustus John, Wyndham Lewis, Alvaro Guevara and probably (for he was fond of sitting for his portrait) by other artists as well; yet it remains extraordinarily difficult to form an exact mental picture of his features. His profile was delicately formed and angular, with a finely-arched nose, a full-lipped mouth and a rather weak chin; his eyes were greyish-blue tending to blue, his hair dark and inclined to be tousled, his complexion fresh, with a rosy tint about the lips and cheek-bones which perhaps owed more to Art than to Nature. (He was in the habit, also, as Mr. C. W. Beaumont testifies,[2] of staining his finger-nails with carmine.) His figure was tall, very slender, and inclined to droop; in his movements, he affected a more-than-feminine *chichi*, walking with a willowy undulation which made him easily (and sometimes embarrassingly) recognizable at a considerable distance. . . . In his clothes he favoured what was conventionally *chic*: dark, well-cut suits, a bowler, gloves and a cane; his physique, however, invested these accoutrements with an element of fantasy, and with his serpentine wriggling, his arch gestures and perpetual giggle, he had the equivocal air of a female impersonator rather than that of a conventional young man about town.

All those who knew him have emphasized Firbank's

[1] *Memoir.*
[2] Quoted by Ifan Kyrle Fletcher (*Memoir*).

extreme shyness: it was, indeed, on social occasions, a matter of considerable difficulty to effect the simplest introduction. Faced by some one he didn't know, Firbank would begin to wriggle and giggle, waving his hands helplessly above his head, spluttering over his words and lapsing finally, in most cases, into complete incoherence. Sometimes he could be monumentally rude—there is a story of how, when he was about to be introduced to some influential personage, he recoiled in horror, exclaiming in an all-too-audible stage-whisper: "My dear, I *couldn't*—he's *far* too ugly!" On another occasion, overcome by the pomposity of an after-dinner speech, he began to giggle uncontrollably, and finally, with his handkerchief stuffed into his mouth, hooting and spluttering with suppressed laughter, was forced to leave the room.

Firbank adored society; yet it must have been a perpetual torture to him. Even with the most congenial of his friends he was apt to be stricken by a sudden onslaught of "nerves." Mr. Augustus John relates[1] how, suddenly encountered one day in Bond Street, Ronald hurried away in alarm, screening his face with his hand, and protesting that he "wasn't fit to be seen." Mr. John adds that "a series of cocktails, a shoot of asparagus, a bottle of wine or two, might have pulled him together." This, as it happens, was precisely the form of treatment which Firbank was wont to prescribe for himself. Like many another neurotic, he doubtless took to alcohol, in the first place, as an escape from his own extreme introversion; before long he became very largely dependent upon it, and his social personality was, in fact, a product of this and other more injurious forms of stimulant. As with others of similar temperament, his extreme timidity would sometimes be replaced, under favourable conditions, by an equally extreme

[1] *Memoir.*

recklessness, and his behaviour on such occasions was apt to shock even the least puritanical of his friends.

One speaks of Firbank's " friends," but the term is to be understood in a specialized sense: it is doubtful if Firbank ever knew the happiness of intimate and lasting friendship. Perhaps he didn't even want it; his extreme aloofness certainly made it difficult, and he would perhaps have preferred, like Wilde, to have been able to say of himself: " I have no friends, only lovers." He was fond, however, of congenial companionship, and had very definite preferences. With women, his shyness became even more paralysing than with men; if his friends insisted upon getting married, Firbank was apt to break off the relationship without explanation or apology.

Timorous and reckless by turns; malicious, hysterical and too apt to flaunt in public (like M. de Charlus) his amorous predilections—Firbank, decidedly, was not well equipped for friendship. Perhaps, too, an additional reason for his aloofness was a fear of becoming too deeply and inconveniently involved. People of Firbank's type are often, in fact, capable of profound and tender affection; and it may be well that Firbank failed in his friendships, not from any native incapacity, but from an unconscious fear that his feeling could never be reciprocated. Also, probably, as Lord Berners suggests, he was " terrified by the idea of being subjected to any tie or obligation." It seems almost certain that the one genuine love of Firbank's life was for his mother. Such men as he are doomed to loneliness, and Firbank seems to have accepted his fate with a certain dignity. Once, it is said, an acquaintance commented, sympathetically, upon his solitary way of life. There is a note of subdued tragedy in Ronald's reply: " I can *buy* companionship."

(IV)

Firbank left Cambridge in June, 1909. By now, it would seem, his family had given up all hope of launching him upon a conventional career, and he himself had abandoned such few definite projects as he had ever cherished—such, for instance, as that of obtaining a post at the Vatican.

In 1910 his father died. There can have been little sympathy between Sir Thomas and his incongruous offspring, and one can, indeed, safely infer that for Ronald his father's death was a blessing in not-very-deep disguise. Not that Sir Thomas had bothered him much (apart from the embarrassing solecism of being an M.P.), but he had had an inconvenient habit of asserting—or trying to assert—his parental authority; he was, moreover, like Mrs. Calvally in *Vainglory*, " one of those destined to get mixed over Monet and Manet all their life." . . . Nor can one suppose that Ronald ignored the fact that his father's death would mean a larger income for himself. . . . As it turned out, this hope was to be disappointed: Sir Thomas had been losing money heavily for some years, and on his death it was revealed that his fortune was but a fraction of what his family had supposed.

Lady Firbank was terrified: ruin stared them in the face. What were they to do? Ronald, faced by the prospect of a clerkship at thirty shillings a week, must have had some *mauvais quarts d'heure*. . . . Fortunately, however, things were not quite so bad as they had appeared at first. The Firbanks found themselves only relatively poor; by ordinary middle-class standards they remained, indeed, very well off.

For a year or two after leaving Cambridge Firbank lived with his mother at her house in Curzon Street. There is no evidence that he was making any very serious attempt to write during this period; no doubt there were too many other things to do. . . . The theatre, for instance—and above all, the Russian Ballet (" I do so *adore* Nijinsky in *Le Spectre de la Rose* "); there was the Post-Impressionist Exhibition at the Grafton Galleries; there were parties; there was the whole intricate and fascinating pageant of late-Edwardian London waiting to be explored. . . . Ronald duly explored it; and it is noteworthy how many of his novels, written at a much later period, hark back to the Edwardian heyday.

His explorations led him into a variety of social territories; for the most part, however, he tended to frequent that equivocal border-country of " Smart Bohemia," which in those days was still a novelty, and which Ronald doubtless found " stimulating " in more ways than one.

He often lunched or dined at the old *Tour Eiffel* in Percy Street, with Augustus John, Thomas Earp or Evan Morgan (subsequently Lord Tredegar). He became a well known and somewhat notorious figure at the Café Royal; and he was often to be found in the bookshop of C. W. Beaumont in the Charing Cross Road. His favourite words at this time were " soothing " and " restful "; he would apply them, indifferently, to a ballet, to a novel by Restif de la Bretonne, to a *bal-musette* in Belleville. . . . His taste for the nineties persisted; he was collecting rare editions of Wilde, Beardsley, Dowson and the rest. It is said, too, that at about this time he became deeply interested in magic, under the influence of Aleister Crowley—though history does not relate how far he progressed in his study of the Black Art; it seems unlikely that the Kabbalah can have held his interest for long, though he may have derived amusement from the works of Eliphas Lévi and those, too, perhaps, of Crowley himself.[1]

[1] There are passing references to this phase in *Vainglory* (see page 58 below).

In 1911 he visited Egypt for the first time; and thenceforward, until the outbreak of war, he travelled widely, visiting Vienna and Constantinople, Rome and Florence; returning always, however, sooner or later, to Paris, which he regarded, without a doubt, as his spiritual home.

For Ronald Firbank, more than for most people, the war when it came must have seemed the ultimate horror. Not for him those heroic thrills (" like swimmers into cleanness leaping ") which, for the more normally constituted of his contemporaries, provided compensation of a kind for the Triumph of Boredom. For Firbank, the war merely meant the end of the only kind of life he liked or was able to cope with. His friends joined up; Lady Firbank, in the prevalent financial scare, feared for her fortune; travel was impossible; there seemed nothing left. . . .

Yet Firbank, ill-equipped as he was to deal with the disaster, was able, after all, to find his own form of compensation. It is not recorded of him that he made even the faintest attempt at " war work." Instead, after spending the first year of the war in London, he retired to Pangbourne, then to Oxford. Here he took rooms in the High, and living in the strictest retirement, without friends in the town or the university, he settled down to write.

Sir Osbert Sitwell has said of Firbank that he was " in the best, the least boring sense of the word, a war-writer."[1] The war, by driving him in upon himself, was in fact responsible for the flowering of his talent. Had he been able to continue indefinitely in his pre-war way of life, it is quite possible— indeed it is probable—that he would never have written anything at all. The act of creation is probably always to

[1] *Memoir.*

some extent a compensatory activity; and certainly it was never more so than in the case of Firbank.

He remained at Oxford, with brief interruptions, for four years. One of his first actions on his arrival had been, symbolically, to change—or at least modify—his name: up till now he had been known, in his family circle and elsewhere, as " Arthur "; henceforward, he announced, he was to be known as " Ronald." *Odette* had been published under the name of " Arthur Firbank "; *Vainglory*, his second published work, appeared in 1915, with a frontispiece by Félicien Rops: upon the title-page is inscribed the name of a " new " author—Ronald Firbank.

(V)

The appearance of *Vainglory* created little stir; none the less, Mr. Grant Richards, the publisher, was persuaded, in the following year, not only to publish the second novel, *Inclinations*, but to reprint *Odette*—though the accompanying story, *A Study in Temperament*, was on this occasion omitted. *Caprice* followed in 1917, with a frontispiece by Augustus John. Meanwhile Firbank began to enjoy a modest—a very modest—celebrity. Mr. Osbert (now Sir Osbert) Sitwell had read a review of *Vainglory*, and, impressed by a quoted fragment, had made it his business to track down the author. He and his brother visited Firbank at Oxford, and subsequently arranged for the publication of a chapter from *Valmouth*, on which he was then engaged, in *Art and Letters*.

For the most part, however, the world remained indifferent to those slim black volumes which now appeared, year by year, from the house of Mr. Grant Richards; or, if not indifferent, somewhat hostile. The intellectual climate was not perhaps propitious for the début of Mrs. Shamefoot or of Miss Sinquier. Indifference or hostility were, indeed, to be expected; Firbank himself was not, perhaps, much surprised. The reviewer for *The Scotsman*, however, provoked a caustic comment—" pleasant, vivacious and stimulating," he wrote of *Inclinations*. " Stimulating to what? " inquired Firbank.

Writing, however, did not absorb his life entirely, and much of his time was spent in reading. Firbank was not an omnivorous reader, but he was, within certain well-defined limits, well-read; during his Oxford period there are signs of a growing seriousness—at least in intention: he was to be seen, during his brief spells in London, at the British Museum reading-room. . . . Was he perhaps studying Egyptology— a subject always near his heart—or the history of magical ritual? Was he preparing, like Mrs. Asp, a study of the " *Women* Queens of England "? He was not: his choice of reading was, in fact, based on an entirely original principle, hitherto unknown within those grave and learned precincts: for he selected his books (we have it on the authority of an onlooker) purely for the beauty of their binding and typography!

The war came to an end at last, and with it Firbank's period of retirement. He returned to London, took rooms in Jermyn Street, and began to seek out his old acquaintances. He was to be seen once more at the Café Royal and at the *Tour Eiffel*; and he became a familiar and indeed a somewhat notorious figure at first-nights.

His behaviour at the theatre was peculiar to say the least: he could only, it appeared, fully enjoy the spectacle by lying recumbent in his seat, his feet in the air, and his head almost touching the floor. . . . The renewal of his social life brought its inevitable accompaniments: he seemed to exist almost

exclusively upon a diet of peaches and champagne, varied
occasionally by a caviare sandwich. His circle of acquaintance
was at this period wide and heterogeneous, and included
such personalities as the Sitwells, Lord Berners, Nina Hamnett,
Wyndham Lewis, Albert Rutherston, C. R. W. Nevinson
and Aldous Huxley (" Aldous—always my *torture*," Ronald
would exclaim, as the author of *Limbo* and *Crome Yellow*
took his seat at the café table).

Valmouth appeared in 1919, and Firbank's celebrity
increased. At the Café Royal he became a well-known
figure, and with his tinted cheeks, his carmined nails and his
shrill, feminine tones, was apt to startle the more conventional
habitués. . . . " My dear," he would suddenly exclaim,
without warning, " I saw a crossing-sweeper in Sloane
Street today with the eyes of a startled faun! "

His passion for the theatre increased, and he determined
to attempt the dramatic form himself. The attempt was
unsuccessful: *The Princess Zoubaroff* (published in 1920)
remains to this day unperformed. At this period, also,
Firbank was developing his cult for the Negro, which partly,
perhaps, grew out of his love for the stage. He frequented
assiduously such shows as *Blackbirds*, and perhaps also was to
be found in less reputable haunts where, to quote his own
words, a closer agreement could be reached upon " the
Eastern problem. . . . "[1] Henceforward the coloured races
were to haunt, ubiquitously, the pages of his novels, culmina-
ting in that highly unconventional study of the West-Indian
negro, *Prancing Nigger*.

In June, 1921, Firbank went to live for some time at
Versailles, where he was working on *The Flower beneath the
Foot*. In the following year he departed for Haiti (" they

[1] See *The Flower beneath the Foot*.

say the President is a *perfect dear* "). For some time previously
he had expressed his intention of going to live in the West
Indies, in order to write a novel about Mayfair; one detects
here an ironic comment upon the conventional idea that the
novelist travels to " gain experience ": a theory which, as
Firbank recognized, is obviously valid only for the literary
journalist, never for the conscious artist.

Firbank visited Haiti, Havana and Barbados; returning to
Europe he took up his quarters first at Bordighera, then at
Rome. His health was failing, and during his brief visits to
London his friends were alarmed for his future welfare. For
one so delicately adjusted, it was obvious that the life he led
was bound to end in a breakdown of some sort; it is even
surprising that he was able to maintain his mental and physical
equilibrium for as long as he did. It was evident that he was
living, as the saying goes, " on his nerves "; he had an extra-
ordinary psychic resilience, and it was always a wonder to
his friends that anybody so hopelessly " unpractical " could
travel to such places as Haiti without being fleeced, robbed
or possibly even murdered.

In 1924 Firbank's mother died. It was a great blow to
him, for the whole store of his affection had been lavished
upon her. After her death he returned to Rome; and it
would appear that, far from making any wholesome change
in his habits, he became thereafter more restless, more
completely subordinated to his vices, than before. In the
autumn of 1925 he was back in London, and his friends,
shocked at his appearance, persuaded him to visit a doctor.
The verdict was apparently a grave one, for Firbank was
discovered on the same evening in the Café Royal, very
drunk, and exclaiming hysterically: " I don't want to die! "

Prancing Nigger had appeared in America in 1924, and had

achieved a certain success. It was even suggested, in New York, that the book should be turned into a musical play; Firbank was delighted by the idea, but nothing seems to have come of it. In the autumn of 1925, in Egypt, he was contemplating a novel about New York (which he had never visited); the book would be written at Cairo, and afterwards, perhaps, he would visit New York itself—a method of working which, as we have seen, Firbank considered (and probably rightly) to be quite as good as the more conventional approach.

The trip to New York, however, was not to materialize; nor, alas! was the novel. In spite of his winter in Egypt his health grew worse; he must have known that he was a very sick man, but still he refused to give way. He continued to work on the New York novel, and wrote frequent reports on its progress to Brentano's, the American publishers. In the spring of 1926 he returned to Rome, where his health gave increased cause for anxiety. Lord Berners was living in Rome at the time, and has described Firbank's last weeks in a sympathetic essay.[1] Up till a few days before his death Firbank continued to live his "normal" life; he did not, according to Lord Berners, seem in worse health than usual. He was taken ill suddenly, one night at his hotel, but appears to have rallied, for the doctor's report, when Lord Berners telephoned to inquire, was satisfactory. A fresh attack must have followed shortly afterwards, for by the next morning Firbank was dead.

He died on May 21, 1926, and was buried by an oversight in the Protestant cemetery; later, when it was discovered that he was a Catholic, his remains were disinterred and reburied in the Catholic cemetery of San Lorenzo.

[1] Included in Ifan Kyrle Fletcher's *Memoir*.

The muddle over Ronald's funeral arrangements was characteristic; in his death, as in his life, an air of vagueness and ambiguity surrounded him. Though the facts of his life are sufficiently well documented, Firbank remains, to a great extent, mysterious. Lord Berners, who knew him, perhaps, better than most people, confesses that he found him perpetually elusive: he refused to drop the mask, even for a moment, and however sympathetic the approach, all efforts to pierce his reserve were firmly, if obliquely, repulsed. His reply to any direct question was invariably the same: " I *wonder!* "

The words might serve, perhaps, not unsuitably, for his epitaph.

CHAPTER II

JUVENILIA AND THE EARLY WORKS
(1905–1915)

(I)

HERE are two characteristic passages from Firbank, both, as it happens, opening paragraphs:

" In the long summer evenings, when the shadows crept slowly over the lawn, and the distant towers of the cathedral turned purple in the setting sun, little Odette d'Antrevernes would steal out from the old grey chateau to listen to the birds murmuring ' Good-night ' to one another amongst the trees . . . "

" Neither her Gaudiness the Mistress of the Robes nor her Dreaminess the Queen were feeling quite themselves. In the Palace all was speculation. Would they be able to attend the *Fêtes* in honour of King Jotifa, and Queen Thleeanhouee of the Land of Dates? Court opinion seemed largely divided. Countess Medusa Rappa, a woman easily disturbable, was prepared to wager what the Countess of Tolga 'liked' (she knew), that another week would find the Court shivering beneath the vaulted domes of the Summer Palace. . . . "

The first of these passages is from *Odette d'Antrevernes* (1905), the second from *The Flower beneath the Foot* (1923). The contrast is instructive: the *Odette* passage might have been written by almost anybody, that from the later novel could have been written by nobody but Ronald Firbank. It is a matter for some surprise that Firbank was willing to republish *Odette* after the appearance of *Vainglory*; he appears, indeed, to have repented of his decision, for, as Sir Osbert

Sitwell tells us,[1] he wished it to be thought, at a slightly later date, that *Vainglory* was his first published work.

Odette is sub-titled " A Fairy Story for Weary People," but one feels that weariness, in this case, has begun at home. It is an extraordinarily feeble effort for a writer of Firbank's talent, and indeed would scarcely pass muster in the more enterprising type of school magazine. It is plainly written under Maeterlinck's influence, and perhaps, too, as Sir Coleridge Kennard has suggested,[2] under that of Francis Jammes. But Firbank conspicuously fails to achieve either the *faux-naïveté* of Jammes or the esoteric simplicities of Maeterlinck: *Odette* has the embarrassing archness of the worst kind of fairy tale, and the hints of the *au-delà* suggest, if anything, an amateur production of Peter Pan. The prose has a coy, girlish sentimentality combined with a kind of decadent piety: one is reminded, irresistibly, of those sickly little " Holy Pictures " which are circulated among Catholic school children.

Briefly, *Odette* is concerned with the experience of a pious little girl who prays that she may, like Ste. Bernadette, be vouchsafed a vision of the Holy Virgin. She manages at last to convince herself that the Madonna will appear to her at midnight in the rose garden. Stealing out to the appointed place, she encounters, instead of the Madonna, " a woman with painted cheeks and flaming hair," lying exhausted by the roadside. Odette comforts her, gives her a silver cross, and sets her on her way:

"But Odette felt somehow changed since last she passed the castle gates. She felt older. For suddenly she realized that life was not a dream . . . that beyond the beautiful garden in which

[1] See Sir Osbert's essay included in Mr. Kyrle Fletcher's *Memoir*.
[2] In his Introduction to *The Artificial Princess*.

she dwelt, many millions of people were struggling to live, and sometimes in the struggle for live one failed—like the poor woman by the river bank."

And so on. It is easy to smile at such a passage coming from the future author of *Valmouth*; easy, too, to dismiss *Odette* as a youthful indiscretion, product of a brief " phase " which Firbank soon " grew out of " and wished forgotten. Yet the awkward fact remains that he apparently thought well enough of *Odette* to republish it more than a decade after its first appearance—in the same year as *Inclinations*.

It would be charitable to conclude that the reissue of *Odette* was a mere oversight on the author's part; but the truth, I believe, is quite otherwise: Firbank, it seems to me, never did entirely " grow out of " his *Odette* phase. *Odette* represented a *genre* in which he would have liked to excel, and for this reason he probably retained for it a sentimental attachment which partially blinded him to its faults. I have compared Firbank's later manner to a child let loose in the old-clothes chest; in *Odette,* I think, one encounters the child without disguise—a naïvely romantic but painfully shy child, who has yet to discover the riches concealed in the chest. Firbank, one feels, wanted to write like Maeterlinck, would have liked, perhaps, to be a wholly " serious " writer; partly from shyness, however, partly from distrust of his own talent, he became, instead, a comedian. (For a timid child it is always less embarrassing to " dress-up " and play the fool than to recite *The Wreck of the Hesperus*.)

Odette, in fact, represents the " romantic " element in Firbank which, weak and ineffectual as it seems in this undiluted form, will reappear as an essential feature of his later manner. We shall encounter it again and again in the works of his maturity: blended adroitly into his more fantastic passages, "jazzed" and parodied, but always recognizable. I have referred already to the "contrapuntal" quality of Firbank's mature style—the synthesis of those two opposed tendencies which gives his prose its peculiar flavour; in *Odette*, I think, one can identify one of these tendencies (and not the least important) in its pure state.

(One could give many instances of phrases and sentences in *Odette* which, at a later date, Firbank would have delighted to pervert or parody. The phrase " wee mite," for instance— in *Odette* it occurs in all seriousness; one can imagine with how different an intention Firbank would have employed it in his later novels.)

Odette d'Antrevernes was first published (under this title) by Elkin Mathews in 1905; the thin, paper-covered volume included also a short sketch, *A Study in Temperament*. *Odette d'Antrevernes* was republished (under the abbreviated title of *Odette*) by Grant Richards in 1916, with four Beardsleyesque illustrations by Albert Buhrer; in this edition the accompanying story was omitted, and has never been reprinted.

A Study in Temperament shows the first hint of Firbank's later manner: not a very revealing hint, but at least the story is an attempt at comedy, and Firbank has abandoned the attempt to write like Maeterlinck. The *Study* is, in fact, a feeble pastiche of Wilde:

" To be smart is to be artificial. To be artificial is to be smart . . . "

Such " epigrams " abound, exploding with a muffled pop like the dampest of damp squibs. The phrase " wee mite " occurs again, embarrassingly. The following passage, however, strikes a new note—the first faint indication of the direction which Firbank was to take:

" ' I think I shall dye my hair *very* gradually to red,' she said. ' I am so tired of gold; of course those yellow tea roses match

D

beautifully, but I think that yellow is becoming monotonous!' She got up and went to a little table covered with books, and picked up a small volume bound in grey. 'A touch of grey will improve my dress,' she thought. . . .

" Lady Agnes opened the book, and found it was one of Maeterlinck's plays.

"'It is so delightful to be seen reading Maeterlinck! So decadent!' . . ."

It is feeble enough—Wilde-and-water would be a not unfair description. The writing is loose and unmuscular—we are a long way still from the close-textured, economical prose of *Vainglory*. Yet Lady Agnes, one feels, does bear a recognizable relation to Firbank's later heroines. And the remark: " I don't know which looked the redder, the women or the roses! " occurs again, with only a slight alteration, in *Vainglory* (p. 35).

One notes Firbank's early addiction to fantastic names: Mrs. Corba, Hester Q. Tail (an American poetess). Here and there, too, one comes upon snatches of dialogue which have almost the authentic Firbankian ring:

"' . . . But tell me, *dear* Mrs. Corba, are you *the* Mrs. Corba?' " Mrs. Corba looked alarmed. . . ."

To approximately this period belong two unpublished pieces by Firbank: a story called *True Love* and a play, *The Mauve Tower*. The typescripts of both these works were examined by Mr. Kyrle Fletcher, from whose remarks one judges that they are not of any great importance.[1] Other unpublished works may, for all one knows, be mouldering somewhere in cupboards and in bottom-drawers; such, until 1934, was the fate of *The Artificial Princess*. It seems unlikely, though, that Firbank—not a very prolific writer, and not always very self-critical—can have left much of his work unpublished.

[1] I have unfortunately been quite unable to gain access to these typescripts, which before the war were in the possession of a London bookseller. Most probably they have perished as a result of enemy action.

(II)

Reckoned by its publication date, *The Artificial Princess* is Firbank's last novel; it appeared posthumously in 1934, eight years after the author's death.[1]   In his introduction, Sir Coleridge Kennard explains that the MS. was put away and " forgotten," and only retrieved during Firbank's last visit to London.   Firbank himself was uncertain whether or not to publish it, realizing that he had used much of the material in his later work; the MS. was sent to Lord Berners, who passed it on to Sir Coleridge after Firbank's death.

The Artificial Princess was, in fact, written at some period prior to *Vainglory*, and must therefore be considered as an early work. I have referred already (page 12) to the curious method by which Firbank amassed his material. Sir Coleridge Kennard tells us that, as early as 1906 (the year after *Odette*), Firbank had begun to hoard the little slips of paper inscribed with isolated phrases and sentences, which he would draw on for his subsequent books.[2] One cannot tell at what date the *Princess* was in fact begun, but it is clear that Firbank was dissatisfied with it as a whole, and used many passages from it in the composition of *Vainglory*. A number of phrases, sentences and even whole paragraphs are transferred to the later book, so different in its general character; and the " Ruritanian " setting recurs in *The Flower beneath the Foot*.

The act of writing, for Firbank, was far from being spontaneous, and though he never appears laboured, his method of working was, in fact, extremely laborious. Every page was worked over again and again, the store of phrases

[1] *The Artificial Princess.* By Ronald Firbank. With an Introduction by Sir Coleridge Kennard. Duckworth, 1934.

[2] I have referred already (page 50) to a passage in *A Study in Temperament* (1905) which recurs in *Vainglory* (1915).

and remarks (kept carefully locked in his desk) was ransacked for suitable interpolations. Firbank's prose, in fact, is an extremely complicated mosaic, built up from a hoard of fragments to which, individually, one can assign no definite date. Moreover, he had a way (as with the *Princess*) of laying aside the work on which he was engaged and starting something else; later, the discarded MS. would be revised and in some cases published. It is therefore impossible to classify Firbank's novels, as one can those of most writers, according to a definite chronological plan.

The Artificial Princess marks a complete break with the manner of *Odette*: the perverse humour, the fantastic characters, the sly innuendo which characterize Firbank's mature work, are already present, though they will be developed very much more fully in *Vainglory*. One suspects that the *Princess* was written with greater speed and spontaneity than the later books; Firbank had at last, one feels, discovered himself, and the discovery had gone slightly to his head. The book is, in fact, rather weak and " diluted " in parts, and it seems likely that Firbank felt, when it was finished, that he had dissipated a lot of good material which could be worked up into something better and more concentrated.

The " story," such as it is, deals with the life of the Court in some imaginary eastern-European capital. Baroness Rudlieb, companion to the Princess, is charged with a mission to a local saint, whom the Princess, in emulation of Salomé, wishes to invite (in the rôle of John the Baptist) to a fête at the Palace; the Baroness, instead of discharging her mission, arranges a rendezvous with her lover; the Saint, nevertheless, arrives for the fête; there are fireworks and a performance of a play by the Mistress of the Robes ("I wrote the play between dinner and prayers "). Nothing " happens," there

is no climax, the incidents as they recur are swept aside by
the incessant stream of dialogue:

> " ' To-morrow,' the Queen went on, ' we will begin our econo-
> mies. The Court shall have Rabbits for dinner. So good for them.'
> " ' Nonsense! ' growled the King, who looked like a tired Viking
> under an elaborate arrangement of jewels. ' It is bourgeois to think
> seriously about one's food; but if you meditate economy, let it not
> be in the *Cuisine*, Madam, for we forbid it,' and with a look of
> fixed horror he stared up into the hollow of the moon, murmuring
> ' Rabbit ' in a deranged voice, as if it were a plot, or the name of a
> poison."

Notice that " tired Viking ": in *The Flower beneath the Foot*,
King William of Pisuerga is described as looking like " a
tired pastry cook "—surely an improvement.

Similarly, the lines by a " Court Poet," beginning " I am
disgusted with Love " (page 68[1]), are used with far better
effect in *Vainglory*, where they are attributed to Mrs. Cresswell,
the Ashringford anchoress. Again, the account of St. Aurora
de Vauvilliers in the *Princess* (page 49) will be developed and
improved in the corresponding sketch of St. Automona di
Meris in *Valmouth*. Firbank, like Norman Douglas, had a
taste for such thumb-nail hagiography, and St. Aurora and
St. Automona can, I think, be derived, through a series of
blasphemous metamorphoses, from the Sunday-school piety
of little Odette d'Antrevernes.

(III)

Vainglory, published in 1915 by Grant Richards, with a
frontispiece by Félicien Rops, may be said to mark Firbank's
début as a mature novelist. Yet one cannot say of it that it
is a typical work; the manner of the *Princess* is largely
abandoned, to be revived and developed at a later stage, but

[1]Page references are to the original edition (Duckworth, 1934).

Vainglory differs as much from the subsequent novels as from its prentice predecessor. It stands by itself in the Firbankian canon: some critics have even considered it his best work, and whether one agrees or not, there is no doubt that it is one of his most attractive.[1]

It is Firbank's longest novel: diffuse, overcrowded, with even less " plot " than usual; parts of it are clumsy and even " difficult "; Firbank's laborious method of " building-up " his prose is already abundantly in evidence; yet there is a lyrical quality about much of the writing which gives *Vainglory* the peculiar and evanescent charm so often possessed by " early works."

The book is designed as a series of set-pieces, and the thread of narrative which connects them is so thin that, at a first reading, one is apt to be irritated and sometimes baffled.

" In style—he was often called obscure, although, in reality, he was as charming as the top of an apple-tree above a wall. . . . "

Thus Firbank aptly describes[2] the work of " Claud Harvester," plainly his own *alter ego*—adding, as though with prophetic intuition of his own future as an author: " His books were watched for . . . but without impatience."

Vainglory is largely set in late-Edwardian London, and is perhaps closer to " real life " than any of the other novels, with the exception of *Prancing Nigger*. The closeness, of course, is relative—the world of which Firbank writes is never any but his own, but there are occasions when his characters do come within measurable distance of reality, and this tendency is more marked in *Vainglory* than elsewhere. Firbank seldom attempted direct social satire, and when he

[1]In the recent reprint, *Five Novels by Ronald Firbank* (Duckworth, 1949), *Vainglory* is, surprisingly, omitted—preference being given to *The Artificial Princess*.

[2]*Vainglory*, page 17.

did (as in the portraits of diplomats in *The Flower beneath the Foot*) he was nearly always unsuccessful. Here, however, the satirical note is just right: the *décor* and the characters remain wholly Firbankian, yet certain parts of London will always, for the Firbank-addict, be haunted by the scenes and personages of *Vainglory*. Who, for instance, can pass Buckingham Palace without recalling that wedding-cake which was to be " an exact replica of the Victoria Memorial "; or has failed to search for the spot " just at the beginning of Sloane Street," where, " under the name of Monna Vanna, Mrs. Shamefoot kept a shop "?

The characters pullulate bewilderingly in the book; the " plot," if one can call it that, is a tangle of sub-plots, none of them very important—a mere scaffolding supporting a vast, rococo-Gothic superstructure. The least obscure motif is perhaps that of Mrs. Shamefoot, whose sole ambition it is to commemorate herself (while still living) by a stained-glass window in a cathedral—" to be caught " (to quote her own words) " in a brutality of stone." She pesters one Bishop after another, and finally decides upon Ashringford where, by a merciful provision of Nature, the Cathedral is finally struck by lightning, thus enabling her to attain at last, by a substantial contribution to the " rebuilding " fund, her heart's desire.

The chief impression which the book produces is of a series of overcrowded receptions and parties: the dialogue is incessant, and Firbank achieves some remarkable effects of orchestration. *Vainglory*, more than the other novels, has an unmistakably Edwardian flavour: feather-boas and electric broughams abound, the dialogue itself has a gushing, over-emphatic quality which brilliantly suggests the chatter of some smart drawing-room of the nineteen-hundreds. Firbank was never, perhaps, to achieve anything more spontaneously funny than the party (near the beginning) given by Mrs. Henedge, to celebrate the discovery of an original fragment of Sappho:

> " ' With a tiara well over her nose, and dressed in oyster satin and pearls, she wished that Sappho could have seen her then. . . . ' "

The guests arrive—Miss Compostella (" nobody would have guessed her to be an actress, she was so private-looking "); Mr. Sophax, Mrs. Asp, Mrs. Thumbler, Mrs. Steeple, Claud Harvester, Winsome Brookes, Mrs. Shamefoot. . . . For dinner, since the occasion is a Sapphic one, there is Lesbian wine (" from Samos. Procured perhaps in Pall Mall. . . . "). Presently Professor Inglepin declaims the " imperishable line " —in the original Greek.

> " ' Will anyone tell me what it means,' Mrs. Thumbler queried, ' in plain English? ' . . .
> " ' In plain English,' the Professor said, with some reluctance, ' it means: " Could not for the fury of her feet! " '
> " ' Do you mean she ran away? '
> " ' Apparently! ' . . . "

One may note, too, Firbank's sly, oblique method of introducing his characters. Here, for instance, is Mrs. Shamefoot:

> " Mrs. Shamefoot, widely known as ' Birdie,' and labelled as politics, almost compels a tear. Overshadowed by a clever husband, and by an exceedingly brilliant mother-in-law, all that was expected of her was to hold long branches of mimosa and eucalyptus leaves as though in a dream at meetings, and to be picturesque, and restful and mute."

And here is a minor character, Mrs. Steeple:

> " One burning afternoon in July, with the thermometer at 90, the ridiculous woman had played *Rosmersholm* in Camberwell. Nobody had seen her do it, but it was conceivable that she had been very fine. . . . "

And Monsignor Parr:

" Something between a butterfly and a misanthrope, he was temperamental, when not otherwise . . . employed."

Firbank is a master of innuendo; those three dots imply the whole of Kraft-Ebing and Havelock Ellis—and even (as Firbank might have added) more.

Most of these characters reappear in *villegiatura* at the cathedral town of Ashringford, where Mrs. Shamefoot is busy with negotiations for her commemorative window:

" ' What are those wonderfully white roses? ' Mrs. Shamefoot inquired of the Bishop, as she trailed with him away.

" In a *costume de cathédrale*, at once massive and elusive, there was nostalgia in every line.

" ' They bear the same name as the Cathedral,' the Bishop replied: ' St. Dorothy.'

" Mrs. Shamefoot touched the episcopal sleeve.

" ' And that calm wee door? ' she asked.

" ' It's the side way in.'

" ' Tell me, Doctor Pantry, is there a ray of hope? '

" ' Without seeming uncharitable, or unsympathetic, or inhuman, what am I to say? With a little squeezing we might bury you in the precincts of the Cathedral.'

" ' But I don't want to be trodden on.' . . . "

In his use of dialogue, Firbank has travelled a long way from *A Study in Temperament*—and even from *The Artificial Princess*. In the above passage the two speakers are perfectly characterized—Mrs. Shamefoot all gushing and ecstatic, the Bishop unctuously clerical. Note the phrase " calm wee door," which Firbank might once (in *Odette*) have used quite seriously; here its effect is purely satirical, and, to drive the point home, as it were, Mrs. Shamefoot's affectation is abruptly quenched by the Bishop's very *terre-à-terre* retort: " It's the side way in."

New characters continually pop up in the already overcrowded cast—Lady Anne Pantry; Miss Wookie; Miss

Compostella's maid Sumph ("'Where's your wedding ring?'
she says. 'I never wear it,' I replied. 'It makes one's hand
look so bourgeoise.' . . . "); Miss Hospice, secretary to Lady
Anne who had discovered her "lost in the advertisements of
The Spectator":

> "With a rather cruel yellow at her neck, waist and feet, and a
> poem of fifty sheets, on *Verlaine at Bournemouth* at her back. What
> is there left to say?"

What indeed? One only wishes that other novelists
possessed more of Firbank's concision.

Here are Lady Anne and her sister-in-law discussing the
new curate:

> "'Probably a creature with a whole gruesome family?' she
> indirectly inquired.
> "'Unhappily, he's only just left Oxford.'
> "'Ah, handsome, then, I hope.'
> "'On the contrary, he's like one of those cherubs one sees on
> eighteenth-century fonts with their mouths stuffed with cake.'
> "'Not really?'
> "'*And he wears glasses.*'
> "'But he takes them off sometimes?'
> "'That's just what I don't know.'"

(Noteworthy is Firbank's adroit use of italics—an aspect of
his style which has been borrowed, consciously or otherwise,
by Mr. Evelyn Waugh.)

One notices, in *Vainglory*, several echoes of Firbank's
interest in Black Magic:

> ". . . 'Do you know, if I stopped here long, I'd start a Satanic
> Colony in your midst just to share the monotony.'
> "'My dear, there's one already.' . . ."

There is, in fact, at Ashringford, a distinct undercurrent of
diabolism, which seems to have affected even the cathedral
architecture:

> "Miss Missingham, in her *Sacerdotalism and Satanism*, has called
> the whole thing heavy, '*Very weighty indeed*,' although she willingly

admits that at twilight the towers, with their many pinnacles, become utterly fantastic, *like the helmets of eunuchs in carnival time*."

The operative phrase here is " she willingly admits," which has just the right note of bogus scholarship. Firbank was fond of quoting, with a solemn pedantry, from such imaginary authorities (there are several instances in *Valmouth*); he slips them in with a deceptive plausibility, one is almost taken off one's guard, as one is with his biographies of saints. One can only hope that some earnest student of the future will compile a complete Firbankian hagiology, and a catalogue of the " works " from which he quotes.

CHAPTER III

THE MIDDLE PERIOD
(1916–1921)

(I)

THE development of Firbank's style cannot, as we have seen, be traced by any reference to the publication dates of his books; sometimes a novel would be laid aside and rewritten; sometimes (one suspects) Firbank was writing two books simultaneously; and always the desk full of fragments, dating back to 1905 or thereabouts, was being drawn upon, so that a late novel such as *Cardinal Pirelli* (published in 1926), may, for all one knows, contain passages written twenty years before.

I emphasize this point merely to excuse the arrangement of this book: such terms as " middle period " or " last period " are used for convenience, and refer merely to the chronological sequence in which Firbank's works appeared.[1]

Inclinations appeared in 1916, with two drawings by Firbank's friend Albert Rutherston. " He pounces down," says Mrs. Asp of Claud Harvester in *Vainglory*, " on those mysterious half-things . . . and sometimes he fixes them! " Like his *alter ego*, Firbank sometimes " fixes " his quarry, sometimes not; in *Inclinations* his hand seems a great deal less steady than usual: over and over again he misfires, and lapses into flatness and silliness. He does it now and again in most

[1] In following this plan, I have made an exception of *The Artificial Princess* which, though it appeared in 1934, is known to have been written before *Vainglory*.

of his books; at his best, he is an unequal writer; but *Inclinations* falls flat from the beginning, and such " plums " as it contains are few and far between.

It is possible that I have a " blind spot " where this novel is concerned; for *Inclinations* has been highly praised, critics have spoken of the " delicacy" of its design and so on. Firbank himself seems to have thought well of it, since he singles it out for mention (together with *Valmouth*) in *The Flower beneath the Foot*. On the other hand, he appears to have been not altogether satisfied with it as a whole, since he took the trouble to rewrite one of the chapters nine years after the book's publication.[1] My own standard of judgment, where Firbank is concerned, is based largely on the fact that his novels are the perfect books to dip into; once familiar with them, one seldom reads them straight through, and in most cases the texture is concentrated enough to make such " dipping " an easy task: one can open (for instance) *Valmouth* or *Vainglory* at almost any page, and be certain of finding a passage one likes. On this principle, I find *Inclinations* the least attractive of the novels; it is the last I would choose from the shelf, and if subjected to what Mr. Wyndham Lewis has called the " taxi-driver's test," it proves (at any rate to my taste) the least rewarding.

Miss O'Brookomore (" authoress of *Six Strange Sisters, Those Gonzagas,* etc.") takes as her companion, on a trip to Athens, a girl " not quite fifteen," Miss Mabel Collins. Miss Collins, who is presented as an almost moronic *ingénue*, elopes with an Italian count, and later returns to her family in England, complete with a " bambino " and a stock of Italian phrases. That is all; as a framework for a novel it is no

[1] *Inclinations*, Part II, Chapter IV. The new version is dated " Rome, April, 1925," and is included, together with the original draft, in the Rainbow edition (1929).

better and no worse than any other of Firbank's—it is unfair,
indeed, to outline the " story " of any of his books. But in
Inclinations the narrative assumes a more than ordinary
importance, because the superstructure of dialogue, which is
the essence of a Firbank novel, is itself so thin in texture:

> " ' Is that you, Mabel? ' she asked.
> " ' How's the poor head? '
> " ' I've been drowsing.'
> " ' I'm glad you could manage that.'
> " ' Isn't the band *awful?* '
> " ' Boom, boom, boom.'
> " ' Did you have a nice time? '
> " ' I've found out one or two things by going down! ' " etc.

It would be hard to find, in any other Firbank novel, such
a banal passage as this. Elsewhere in the book Firbank lapses
into a hysterical, exclamatory manner which is exceedingly
irritating:

> " ' There's an arrival,' she said.
> " ' Oh! '
> " ' What is it? '
> " ' He's here! '
> " ' Oh! Mabel '
> " ' Oh! Gerald! '
> " ' Oh! Mabel! '
> " ' Oh! Gerald! ' . . . "

And there is, of course, the famous Chapter XX which I
may as well quote in full (it follows the elopement of the
heroine):

> " ' Mabel! Mabel! Mabel! Mabel!
> " ' Mabel! Mabel! Mabel! Mabel! ' "

Inclinations is a puzzling affair altogether; coming after the
highly-wrought tapestry of *Vainglory* its thinness and poverty
of invention are astonishing. One can only conclude that
Vainglory had, for the time being, exhausted Firbank's not
very robust talent; *Inclinations* bears all the marks of having
been written, like the play in *The Artificial Princess*, " between

dinner and prayers "; its prose suggests the facile " strumming " of some tired pianist, recuperating from the strain of a début. Sometimes his fatigue overcomes him completely, and he bangs his fist down in a defiant discord, *pour épater le bourgeois*—as, for instance, in Chapter XX quoted above, which is the purest Dadaism.

It is interesting to compare the two versions of the rewritten chapter already referred to. The second draft, composed a decade after the first, is considerably improved; the texture is thickened, the innuendo more pointed: it is the manner of *Valmouth* and *Pirelli*. The most charitable thing one can say about *Inclinations* is that Firbank was trying, perhaps, to write more simply and directly—possibly, for all one knows, at the suggestion of his publisher. If this was indeed the case, he seems soon to have abandoned the attempt, and his tendency, in subsequent books, is towards a greater complexity of design. Firbank was never, one feels, very self-critical, and he remained, till the end of his career, capable of astonishing lapses into feebleness and silliness (his next book, *Caprice*, includes several); but he was never again to write quite so badly as in *Inclinations*.

Yet even *Inclinations* has its moments—as in Miss O'Brookomore's comment on the dance-band in the hotel at Athens:

" ' It sounds like the Incest-Music,' she murmured, ' to some new opera! ' "

Or her maid's enterprising query during the voyage out:

" ' When Greek meets Greek, miss,' she asked informingly, ' can you tell me what they're supposed to do? '

" ' Since we're all English,' Miss O'Brookomore replied, ' I don't think it matters.' . . . "

Note, by the way, the illiterate use of the word " informingly." Firbank would never, one feels, have passed the

School Certificate. His spelling is as faulty as his grammar: he will write "ingenious" for "ingenuous," and although he was by all accounts a competent linguist, his French and Italian phrases are more often than not inaccurate.

(II)

Caprice, the next novel, appeared from Grant Richards in 1917 (the same year, incidentally, as *South Wind*), with a frontispiece by Augustus John. Like *Inclinations*, it is concerned with an *ingénue* launched suddenly upon Society: in this case, the stage-struck daughter of a country clergyman, who, bearing her godmother's pearls and most of the family plate, escapes to London with the firm intention of becoming a famous actress. (This "innocent abroad" theme occurs over and over again in Firbank: first stated in *Odette*, it is taken up in *Inclinations* and *Caprice*, recurs in a somewhat altered aspect in *The Flower beneath the Foot*, and emerges once again, for the last time, in *Prancing Nigger*.)

The arrival of Sarah Sinquier in London is a justly famous episode; finding that Mrs. Bromley, the theatrical agent with whom she has an appointment, has inconsiderately died on the previous night, she seeks refreshment in "some nice teashop, some cool creamery. . . ."

> "How did this do?
> "'The Café Royal!'
> "Miss Sinquier fluttered in . . .
> "'Bring me some China tea,' she murmured to a passing waiter, 'and a bun with currants in it.' . . .'"

But sitting opposite to her at the table, she observes "an adolescent of a sympathetic, somewhat sentimental, appearance, who, despite emphatic whiskers, had the air of a wildly pretty girl."

And before she has time to consider she is launched into Bohemia:

> " Here were stage folk, artists, singers. . . . "

She becomes the *protegée* of a Mrs. Sixsmith, a lady of highly dubious connections, theatrical and otherwise, who offers to dispose of Sarah's pearls and silver " through an old banker friend of mine—Sir Oliver Dawtry." Other café habitués emerge: Mr. Ernest Stubbs, " whose wild wanderings in the Gog-Magog hills in sight of Cambridge, orchestrally described, recently thrilled us all "; Harold Weathercock and Noel Nice; Miss Whipsina Peters, " a daughter of the famous flagellist—and a coryphée herself." The banker-friend disposes of the pearls, Mrs. Sixsmith takes her commission, and assumes the rôle of impresario:

> " ' I will find you actors—great artists.' . . .
> " ' Oh, God ! ' . . . Miss Sinquier's eyes shone. . . .
> " ' I'll have that boy.'
> " ' What—what boy? '
> " ' Harold Weathercock.'
> " ' You desire him? '
> " ' To be my Romeo, of course.' . . . "

There is a convivial dinner with Sir Oliver:

> " ' I notice Miss Peters here tonight,' he said.
> " ' Whipsina? '
> " ' With two young men.'
> " ' Un trio n'excite pas de soupçons, they say.'
> " ' They do. . . . ' "

A theatre is taken, the " Source " (with a well beneath the stage); Miss Sinquier makes her *début*—as Juliet. It is her hour of glory:

> " ' Her acting is a revelation ' . . . ' there has been nothing like it for years.' . . . ' An unfeminine Juliet.' . . . ' A decadent Juliet.' . . . ' The Romeo kiss—you take your broadest fan.' . . . 'A distinctive revival.' . . . ' Shakespeare as a Cloak.' "

E

"Oh God! How quite . . . delicious!" exclaims the new Juliet, transported by the reviews. . . . Alas, for fame—Miss Sinquier, imprudently exploring the empty theatre on the morning after her *début*, trips over a mousetrap and falls into the well beneath the stage.

Caprice, in one sense, is Firbank's most " conventional " novel; it has a very definite " story," which moves to its appointed end without too many interruptions, and without the top-heavy superstructure of dialogue which, for the new-comer to Firbank, is apt to make his work seem " difficult." *Caprice*, in fact, succeeds where *Inclinations* fails—though here again there is an irritating vein of silliness, the dialogue tends at moments to become vapid and exclamatory; Firbank was not at his best, I think, with *ingénue* heroines (or not, at any rate, with white ones; with negresses, as we shall see in *Prancing Nigger*, he was more successful). One reason for this, perhaps, is that these *jeunes filles en fleur* are very largely projections of Firbank himself: he, too, was in a sense an " innocent abroad," an easy prey to the world's rapacity and cruelty, and his heroines reflect his own frustrated longings, the bitterness and the hidden tragedy of *l'amour qui n'ose pas dire son nom*. For anybody as exquisitely self-conscious as Firbank it was an agony to write about himself—even under the dis-guise of Miss Sinquier or Laura de Nazianzi; hence the irritating coyness, the silliness, the innumerable exclamation marks.

Whether or not Miss Sinquier is to some extent a projection of Firbank himself, she certainly reflects his own passion for the theatre. *Caprice* exhales the very smell of grease-paint, it is full of remarks which might almost, one feels, have been overheard at the " Ivy ":

"'And there was the wind bellowing and we witches wailing: and no Macbeth!' a young man with a voice like cheap scent was saying to a sympathetic journalist for whatever it might be worth. . . . "

(III)

Valmouth, which appeared in 1919 (again with a frontispiece by John), has for its sub-title " A Romantic Novel." The label is an apt one: for the whole book is impregnated with a heavy, erotic taint of incense, its atmosphere is as sinister as that of a Gothic romance. One is tempted to say of *Valmouth* that it is by Congreve out of Mrs. Radcliffe.

I think, myself, it is Firbank's masterpiece, far and away better than anything else he wrote. Firbank's admirers are apt to quarrel over their preferences, some of which seem to me unaccountable: I have even, for instance, heard *Inclinations* singled out as a favourite, and many critics have plumped for *The Flower beneath the Foot*. Mr. Forster,[1] on the other hand, seems to prefer *Prancing Nigger*, which is an intelligible choice though one may not agree with it.

My own preference for *Valmouth* may be only a personal idiosyncrasy—it happens to be the novel I most often dip into; but on re-reading it once again, I am more convinced than ever that, on purely technical grounds, it is Firbank's best book. In it, he seems to me to achieve precisely what he sets out to do, and the book has a balance and coherence of design which, in the other novels, is too often lacking. There is an adequate thread of narrative, which is never (as in *Vainglory*) lost sight of; nor does the development of the story lead to flatness and banality (as in *Inclinations*). This equilibrium seems to me unique in Firbank; there are, I know, passages in *Prancing Nigger* or *Cardinal Pirelli* equal (or almost equal) to the best in *Valmouth*; but neither of these later books, considered *as a whole*, seems to me so successful as its predecessor.

[1] *Abinger Harvest*.

Valmouth is set in some imaginary health resort on the West
Coast (" the neighbouring Garden Isles " lie not far off it);
the climate is so salubrious that most of the inhabitants live
to be centenarians, while not a few achieve a considerably
greater longevity (" the last time I went to the play . . . was
with Charles the Second and Louise de Querouaille, to see
Betterton play Shylock. . . . "). The centenarian joke is not
a very good one, and is not particularly important to the
narrative; nor does Firbank over-emphasize it. The " story "
is concerned with the two ancient *douairières* of Hare-Hatch
House, Mrs. Hurstpierpoint and Mrs. Thoroughfare, and
with the anomalous behaviour of the heir, Captain Dick
Thoroughfare, a naval officer with unconventional views
about marriage.

The book opens on a richly romantic note:

> " Day was drooping on a fine evening in March as a brown
> barouche passed through the wrought-iron gates of Hare-Hatch
> House on to the open highway.
>
> " Beneath the crepuscular, tinted sky, the countryside stretched
> away, interspersed with hamlets, meads and woods, towards low,
> loosely engirdling hills, that rose up against the far horizon with a
> fine monastic roll."

This opening passage has a quality of " professional "
assurance which one has not yet met with in Firbank; it is
good " description," the mannerisms are effective but not
too obtrusive (note the alliterations—" Day was drooping,"
" brown barouche "); the note is perfectly set for what is to
follow (even the word " monastic " hints at the book's
prevailing atmosphere); the whole passage, I think, strikes a
perfect balance between romantic sensibility and Firbankian
pastiche.

Thetis Tooke, a farmers' daughter, has conceived a passion

for the heir of Hare, who, however, has become affianced, during his last voyage, to a negress, Niri-Esther, supposed to be a Tahitian princess (Firbank is extremely vague about the nationality of his coloured characters). Niri-Esther arrives at Valmouth, passing as the niece, daughter or (merely) *protégée*—one is never sure which—of Mrs. Yajnavalkya, a negress-masseuse in the town. Captain Dick returns from sea to claim his bride; he is accompanied by his " middy-chum," Jack Whorwood (" that little lad, upon a cruise, is, to me, what Patroclus was to Achilles, and even more "). Thetis Tooke, after attempting suicide, is received into a convent; the union of Dick Thoroughfare and Niri-Esther is celebrated " with all the ferment of a *Marriage-Christening*," for their first-born daughter has anticipated the wedding. . . . There are several sub-plots—Lady Parvula de Panzoust, a visiting centenarian, conducts an abortive liaison with David Tooke (brother of Thetis), assisted by the dubious ministrations of Mrs. Yajnavalkya; Mrs. Hurstpierpoint conceives a passion for Niri-Esther; *Valmouth*, in fact, is a tissue of complex and improbable amours, most of them (and for the best of reasons) implied rather than stated.

Perhaps the most notable character in the book is the *masseuse*, Mrs. Yajnavalkya; indeed, " Mrs. Yaj " is very nearly, if not quite, the best of all Firbank's characters. She bounces through the book with the vitality and robustness of a black Moll Flanders:

> " Niri-Esther's clothes " (she remarks) " . . . are a little too vainglorious! At her age . . . and until I was past eighteen, I nebber had more in de course ob a year dan a bit ob cotton loincloth. You may wear it how you please, my poor mother would say, but dat is all you'll get! And so, dear me, I generally used to put it on my head."

Here is Mrs. Yaj again, indulging in a little Higher Criticism with one of her clients:

> " 'Do you really believe now, Mrs. Tooke my dear, in de Apostolic succession? . . . '
>
> " 'I han't paid any heed lately to those chaps, Mrs. Yaj; I'm going on to Habakkuk.'
>
> " 'Was not he de companion ob de Prodigal Son? '
>
> " 'Maybe he was, my dear. He seems to have known a good many people.'
>
> " 'Dat is not de name now ob a man, Mrs. Tooke, to observe a single wife, nor even a single sex. . . . No! Oh no; a man wif a name like dat would have his needs! ' . . . "

Mrs. Tooke herself is among the more successful of the minor characters. In *Valmouth* Firbank attempts (and brilliantly achieves) among other things a skit on the " rural " novel. Mrs. Tooke and her grandson would not have been out of place on Cold Comfort Farm:

> " 'Since the day my daughter-in-law—Charlotte Carpster that was—died in child-bed, and my great, bonny wild-oat of a son destroyed himself in a fit of remorse, there's been nothing but trouble for me.' . . . "

One of the best chapters in the book describes a dinner-party at Hare-Hatch House. Lady Parvula de Panzoust is discussing the " wondrous orchids " in her own conservatory:

> " 'We're very proud of a rose-lipped one . . . with a lilac beard.'
>
> " 'A lilac . . . *what?* ' It was Mrs. Hurstpierpoint's voice at the door. . . . 'Is it Sodom? ' she enquired, in her gruff, commanding way, coming forward into the room. . . .
>
> " Lady Parvula tittered.
>
> " 'Goodness, no,' she said.
>
> " 'Because Father Mahoney won't hear of it ever *before* dessert.'
>
> " 'How right.'
>
> " 'He seems to think it quite soon enough.' . . . "

Lady Parvula, " exhaling indescribably the esoteric gentil-lezze of love," is one of Firbank's most typical characters, suggesting some fantastic courtesan of the nineties seen through the eyes of Toulouse-Lautrec. Her diffuse, gushing monologues, on the other hand, recall the reminiscences of some decayed Edwardian peeress:

" ' ... One could count more alluring faces out with the Valmouth, my husband used to say, than with any other pack. The Baroness Elsassar—I can see her now on her great mauve mount with her profile of royalty in misfortune—never missed. Neither, bustless, hipless, chinless, did " Miss Bligh "! It was she who so sweetly hoisted me to my saddle when I'd slid a-heap after the run of a " fairy " fox. We'd whiffed it—the baying of the dogs is something I shall never forget; dogs always know!—in a swede-field below your house from where it took us by break-neck, rapid stages—(oh! oh!) —to the sands. There, it hurried off along the sea's edge, with the harriers in full cry; all at once, near Pizon Point, it vanished. Mr. Rogers, who was a little ahead, drew his horse in with the queerest gape—like a lost huntsman (precisely) in the *Bibliothèque bleue*.'

" ' It's a wonder,' " (Mrs. Thoroughfare comments) " ' he didn't vomit.' ... ' "

Firbank is famous for his fantastic names, but he never, I think, hit on better ones than in *Valmouth*. " Funny " names are apt, for most writers, to be a pitfall: they are all very well in Dickens and in Restoration comedy, but in a modern novel one has to use them with economy and discretion. Firbank is not always successful—sometimes the joke is rather obvious, as in " Zenobia Zooker " or " May Heaven " (both from *Valmouth*). Lady Parvula de Panzoust, however, has just the right elaborate and hieratic quality; and Mère Marie de Cœurbrisé (Mother-Superior at the convent), Madame Mimosa (the local courtesan), Mrs. Q. Comedy, Lady Lucy Saunter, Violet Ebbing, Mrs. Thoroughfare, are not only perfectly fitted to their owners, but contrive to be extremely funny without being " obvious."

One cannot leave *Valmouth* without reference to that devastating scene in which Mrs. Hurstpierpoint, prostrated by a thunderstorm, seeks solace in the life of St. Automona di Meris, which her maid reads aloud to her:

"'One day St. Automona di Meris, seeing a young novice yawning, suddenly spat into her mouth, and *that* without malice or thought of mischief. Some ninety hours afterwards the said young novice brought into the world the Blessed St. Elizabeth Bathilde, who, by dint of skipping, changed her sex at the age of forty and became a man.' . . .

"' Is the worst of the storm yet over, Fowler, do you consider? ' " . . . . (Mrs. Hurstpierpoint enquires).

"' Now that the wind has deprived the statues of their fig leaves, 'm . . . I hardly can bear to look out.' . . . "

The invaluable Fowler, in a further attempt to console her mistress, proffers a relic from the reliquary:

"' You used to say the toe, 'm, of the married sister of the Madonna, the one that was a restaurant proprietress (Look alive there with those devilled-kidneys, and what is keeping Fritz with that sweet omelette?), in any fraças was particularly potent.' . . . "

(This sentence, I should say, is probably the most convoluted and certainly one of the funniest in English fiction.)

Finally, one should notice Firbank's elaborate orchestrations of chance-heard phrases : there is a good example in *Vainglory*, at the gathering which celebrates Mrs. Shamefoot's vitrification; there is another and better one in *Valmouth*, at the centenarians' fête at Hare-Hatch House:

"' Heroin.'

"' Adorable simplicity.'

"' What could anyone find to admire in such a shelving profile? '

"' My husband had no amorous energy whatsoever; which just suited me, of course.'

"' I suppose when there's no more room for another crow's-foot, one attains a sort of peace? '

"' I once said to Doctor Fothergill, a clergyman of Oxford and a great friend of mine, " Doctor," I said, " Oh, if only you could see my—— " '

"' *Elle etait jolie! Mais jolie . . . C'était une si belle brune!* ' "

" ' Cruelly lonely.'

" ' Leery . . . '

" ' Vulpine.'

" ' Calumny.'

" ' People look like pearls, dear, beneath your wonderful trees.' . . .

" ' Above social littleness. . . . '

" ' Woman as I am! ' . . .

" ' . . . A Jewess in Lewisham who buys old clothes, old teeth, old plate, old paste, old lace. And gives very good prices indeed.' . . . "

(IV)

I have quoted at some length from *Valmouth*, for my aim in this book, as I have said, is to " present " Firbank rather than to criticize him. Quotation, however, is always an unsatisfactory method, and Firbank's apparent " quotability " is deceptive: his best passages, torn from their context, are liable to wilt like uprooted orchises in a suburban garden. Yet how else can one transmit the quality of a book? I believe *Valmouth* to be Firbank's masterpiece; and having risked so much, I will go further and assert that it is, in fact, one of the key books of its age (roughly the nineteen-twenties), and can claim an honourable place along with *Antic Hay*, *Eminent Victorians*, *To the Lighthouse* and Mr. Eliot's earlier poems.

After *Valmouth* (1919) Firbank published nothing else of importance until 1923. During this period he seems to have been taking stock of his resources, and contemplating more than one new departure. *The Princess Zoubaroff*, a play, appeared in 1920, and *Santal*, a semi-serious novelette, in 1921. Both are failures, but *Zoubaroff*, as Firbank's only attempt (in his maturity) at the drama, is of some interest.

The Princess Zoubaroff: A Comedy has a frontispiece and decorations by Michel Sevier. Its reception was cool: the theatrical world, presumably, remained in ignorance of its existence, and there is no evidence to show that Firbank made any serious effort to get it produced.

This neglect is not surprising; for Firbank, in spite of his lifelong interest in the drama, had even less " theatre-sense " than most novelists. *Zoubaroff* is simply a Firbank novel cut up into acts and scenes, and with the descriptive passages left out. It has been compared with Congreve, but the analogy seems to me unfortunate (though for that matter, almost any artificial comedy in English is apt to be fathered on the Restoration—it is almost a *cliché* of criticism). What Firbank would really have liked to write, one feels, was a *chic* and rather silly social comedy: he was not a highbrow where the theatre was concerned, he enjoyed, like Miss Sinquier, any " light vaudeville or new revue," and probably admired the early comedies of Mr. Noel Coward. The characters in *Zoubaroff* are rather boringly *chic* in the Shaftesbury Avenue sense: they drink cocktails and play billiards, even their names (Eric, Reggie, Enid, etc.) have an un-Firbankian (though doubtless intentional) banality. In the dialogue, too, Firbank aims at a conventional flatness, varied with exclamatory passages in the style of *Inclinations*: one has an uneasy feeling that he is trying to galvanize the play into life by an excessive use of exclamation marks. But the attempt at conventionality is unsuccessful. Firbank is perpetually betrayed into speeches which might have come out of *Valmouth* or *Vainglory*—a weakness which, if it detracts (as indeed it does) from the play's dramatic value, at least makes it more acceptable as a bedside book.

The action takes place in Florence, and the dialogue is sprinkled liberally with Italian phrases. There are numerous subsidiary characters—Lord Orkish, Mrs. Mangrove, Blanche Negress, Monsignor Vanhove: recognizably Firbankian, but cramped and diminished by the medium. They wander in and out, exchanging irrelevant snatches of dialogue:

> "LORD ORKISH: . . . I'm never bored. I enjoy everything.
>
> "REGGIE: So do I too! I love society. Alone with my shadow I'm soon depressed. . . . I and a friend of mine, Claud Cloudley, we've been visiting all the P's . . . Pavia, Parma, Padua, Perugia, Pisa . . .
>
> "PRINCESS: Is it a method?
>
> "REGGIE: Claud's such an extremist, you know. . . . They say when he kissed the Pope's slipper . . . he went on to do considerably more. . . ."

The Princess Zoubaroff herself contributes little to the action, though she is a vehicle for a number of memorable remarks:

> " . . . I am always disappointed with mountains. There are no mountains in the world as high as I could wish. . . . They irritate me invariably. I should like to shake Switzerland."
>
> "I remember he died just as the clock was striking midday. . . . He begged me to mourn him in Chinese fashion—White. . . . And then, when all the wreaths were spread, I danced a *gavotte* over his grave. . . ."

It is a pity, one feels, that Firbank wasted so much promising material in attempting his " comedy "; as a novel, *Zoubaroff* might have been one of his best—even, perhaps, another *Valmouth*. Indeed, there are signs that *Valmouth* still haunted him—the Monsignori, the convents, the preoccupation with " queens " and Sapphism; and Enid's line " It was part of my corbeille " (page 19) occurs also in *Valmouth* (page 37).

Santal, the only other published work of this fallow period, appeared in 1921, in a thin, paper-covered pamphlet of forty-two pages. It is a souvenir of one of Firbank's trips to North Africa—on the last page appears the note: " Algiers, Tunis." *Santal* is a reversion to Firbank's " serious " vein— an attempt to do *Odette* over again on Algiers:

" He rode forward that day with his eyes fixed upon the distant mountain, and in the blue of evening halted for the night in the open plain. There was light enough still to read the Koran (which seemed to hold new meanings among altered surroundings), but the delight of beholding Mount Matmata before him made it difficult to concentrate the mind entirely upon it now. Coiffed with clouds, it had the air of some fabulous mosque . . . " etc.

" Coiffed with clouds "—the Firbankian phrase flashes out of the pedestrian prose: Firbank could never, for long, discard his habitual mannerisms. The passage quoted is characteristic: a carefully wrought, nostalgic realism, which lapses only occasionally into the familiar vein of bawdy innuendo:

" ' Safia, the lately repudiated wife of Abou Zâzaa, takes a Hammam every day! '

" ' She is growing so exotic! '

" ' They say she's in love with a peacock's feather! '

" ' Give me a black moustache,' Amoucha sighed, ' and two passionate legs! ' . . . "

All the characters in *Santal* are Arabs; the hero, a pious youth devoted to the Koran, sets out rather vaguely on a pilgrimage; the book is heavy with the taint of a semi-erotic religious nostalgia. One feels that Firbank, bored by choir-boys and nuns, has been tempted to try Islam for a change. . . . The experiment is not successful; *Santal* is his dullest book, and it is hardly surprising that it has never been reprinted.

CHAPTER IV

THE LAST NOVELS

(1923–1926)

(I)

AFTER a period of experiment (1919–22) Firbank seems to have gained a kind of " second wind," and during the remaining four years of his life wrote with a greater care and assurance than ever before. Three books belong to this period—*The Flower beneath the Foot, Prancing Nigger* and *Concerning the Eccentricities of Cardinal Pirelli*: they contain some of the best of Firbank and are, on the whole (always excepting *Valmouth*), his most satisfactory novels.

The Flower beneath the Foot appeared in 1923, with a decoration by C. R. W. Nevinson and portraits by Augustus John and Wyndham Lewis. At the end of the book appears the inscription: " July 1921, May 1922. Versailles, Montreux, Florence." More than most of Firbank's books, this one conveys the atmosphere of particular places; although its *mise-en-scène* is the imaginary land of " Pisuerga," one recognizes, for instance, Lac Léman (souvenir of his stay at Montreux), and there are a number of descriptive passages which show a greater interest in landscape for its own sake than is usual with Firbank.

It is not his best book (though some people may disagree with this judgment)—Firbank's vein of ninetyish sentimentality (the hangover from *Odette*) is here once again apparent; and the portraits of the Court of St. James at Pisuerga are cheaply libellous and ineffective. (One at least of the diplomats whom he satirizes was to retaliate with a quasi-fictitious study of Firbank which is far more telling than any of Firbank's own essays in the *genre*.) Nevertheless, *The Flower beneath the Foot* is vintage Firbank—if only of the *deuxième cru*. It was always, I believe, one of his most popular novels, and the adjective " Firbankian," in the critics' vocabulary, seems often to refer to the particular world which he here depicts—a fantastic " Ruritania " in which the primitive is contrasted with the decadent: a land of feather-boas and wireless sets, incongruously populated by Edwardian dames, tartan-kilted negroes, queer Monsignori, eccentric diplomats and so on. Mr. Evelyn Waugh perhaps remembered " Pisuerga " when he wrote *Black Mischief*; and several minor imitators of Firbank have staked out a claim there, though none that I know of has succeeded perfectly in acclimatizing himself.[1]

The leading *motif* in the book is the *liaison* of Laura de Nazianzi, a lady-in-waiting at the Court, with the heir-apparent, His Weariness Prince Yousef. (All the Royal Family of Pisuerga have such titles—Her Dreaminess the Queen, His Naughtiness Prince Olaf, etc. They are well chosen but, I think, introduce an element of whimsy which is unworthy of Firbank.) For the Prince the *affaire* is a passing caprice, for Laura a grand passion; it is frowned upon by the Court, and a marriage is arranged for Prince Yousef with Princess Elsie (daughter of King Geo and Queen Glory) of England. The heart-broken Laura retires to the Convent of the Flaming Hood (a singularly unorthodox institution) where we leave her well on the way to becoming a saint.

[1] *Frolic Wind*, by Richard Oke (Gollancz, 1929), may be singled out as one of the best novels written under Firbank's influence.

(That she was finally canonized is a matter of certainty, for the book has for epigraph a " quotation " from " St. Laura de Nazianzi ": " Some girls are born organically good: I wasn't.")

There are several enticing sub-plots—the intrigues, for example, of Madame Wetme, whose ambition it is to be presented at Court; Queen Thleeanhouee's embarrassing attachment to Lady Something, the English Ambassadress ("' Let us go away by and by, my dear gazelle,' she exclaimed with a primitive smile, ' and remove our corsets and talk '"); an archæological expedition (financed by the Queen) to excavate the ruins of Chedorlahomor, "a *faubourg* of Sodom ":

> " ' It was in the Vale of Akko . . . ' " (to quote the Archæological Society's " initial report ") " ' that we laid bare a superb tear-bottle, a unique specimen in grisaille, severely adorned with a matron's head. From the inscription there can be no doubt whatever that we have here an authentic portrait of Lot's disobedient, though unfortunate, wife. Ample and statuesque (as the salten image she was afterwards to become) . . . it is a face you may often see today, in down-town " Dancings," or in the bars of the dockyards or wharves of our own modern cities . . . a sodden, gin-soaked face that helps to vindicate, if not, perhaps, to excuse, the conduct of Lot.' . . . "

The *vie intime* of the Pisuergan Family Royal is lightly sketched in:

> " ' Whenever I go out,' the King complained, ' I get an impression of raised hats.'
>
> " . . . Doctor Babcock looked perturbed.
>
> " ' Raised hats, sir? ' he murmured in impressive tones.
>
> " ' Nude heads, Doctor.' . . . "
>
> " ' What is the acme of nastiness? ' . . . [the King enquires, on another occasion, of the English Ambassadress, having lunched that day with the local branch of the Girl Guides].
>
> " ' Oh, *la*, sir,' she stammered, ' how should I know? '
>
> " The King looked the shrinking matron up and down. ' The supreme disgust . . . '

" ' Oh *la*, sir!' . . .

" . . . ' Tepid potatoes,' he answered, ' on a cold plate.'

" The Ambassadress beamed.

" ' I trust the warmth of the girls, sir, compensated you for the coldness of the plates? ' she ventured.

" ' The inspection, in the main, was satisfactory.' . . . "

The Queen's *entourage* gives Firbank plenty of scope—Countess Medusa Rappa, the Duchess of Varna, Olga Blumenghast, Countess Yvorra. . . . The intricacies of their amours are hardly rivalled by those of the ladies in *Valmouth;* one eavesdrops perpetually upon their indiscretions:

" ' I would give all my soul to him, Rara . . . my chances of heaven!'

" ' Your chances, Olga . . . ' Mademoiselle de Nazianzi murmured.

" ' How I envy *the men*, Rara, in his platoon!'

" ' Take away his uniform, Olga, and what does he become?'

" ' Ah *what*—— ' . . . Mademoiselle Blumenghast clasped her hands brilliantly across the nape of her neck. . . . ' I want to possess him at dawn, at dawn,' she broke out: ' beneath a sky striped with green.' . . . "

One remembers, too, that portentous figure, Mrs. Montgomery, the Royal Governess:

" ' 'Ow can you be so frivolous, your royal 'ighness? . . . for shame, wicked boy! For shame!' And her cheery British laugh echoed gaily down the corridors. . . . "

Even more British (though distinctly less cheery) is Princess Elsie, the English bride of Prince Yousef:

" ' She called for fried-eggs and butcher's-meat, this morning, about the quarter before eight.' . . .

" ' An excellent augury for our dynasty,' the King declared . . . "

The Royal Marriage is duly celebrated, and the procession is witnessed by Laura (the future saint) from the roof of her convent:

"A burst of cheering seemed to announce the Queen. But no, it was only a lady with a parasol sewn with diamonds that was exciting the rah-rahs of the crowd . . . Madame Wetme was enjoying a belated triumph. And now a brief lull, as a brake containing various delegates and 'representatives of English culture' rolled by at a stately trot—Lady Alexander, E. V. Lucas, Robert Hichens, Clutton-Brock, etc.—the ensemble, the very apotheosis of worn-out *cliché.* . . . "

Prince Yousef and his bride appear at last:

"A shaking of countless handkerchiefs in wild ovation: from roof-tops and balconies the air was thick with falling flowers—the bridal pair!

" But only for the bridegroom had she eyes.

" Oblivious of what she did, she began to beat her hands, until they streamed with blood, against the broken glass ends upon the wall: ' Yousef, Yousef, Yousef.' . . . "

The Flower beneath the Foot is the first of Firbank's novels to end on a tragic note; henceforward, sadness will haunt his final chapters—though in the two remaining novels the tragic element is not allowed to intrude quite so obviously as here. In *The Flower beneath the Foot* Firbank yields to a temptation which has already beset him in earlier works; the last paragraph (quoted above), is a *cri du coeur*—in Laura de Nazianzi, as in Miss Sinquier and Mabel Collins, we see once again an aspect of Firbank himself: the timorous, immature young man beneath the cynic pose, perpetually frustrated, the victim of a love which can never be requited. In *Caprice* he could still resist the temptation to be "serious": Miss Sinquier is not more tragic than, for instance, the Dong with the Luminous Nose. In *Prancing Nigger* and *Pirelli* the "seriousness" is there, but safely hedged about with irony and self-mockery. Once bitten, twice shy: Firbank was not to be seduced a second time into such an embarrassing self-betrayal.

It seems likely that this growing element of sadness had its origin in Firbank's failing health. He realized by now, probably, that he had not many years to live; he had, moreover,

F

reached an age which for persons of his temperament is too often a tragic one: for sexual abnormality, though it may seem a bearable misfortune in youth, is less easy to come to terms with in middle-age. Friendship was never easy for Firbank; and sooner or later most of his friends deserted him: Prince Yousef was bound, in the end, to marry Princess Elsie, he himself was doomed to witness their nuptials (though not without a certain ironic amusement) from behind the conventual bars of his own temperament.

(II)

Firbank's next novel was published (in England) in 1925, under the title of *Sorrow in Sunlight*; it had already appeared in New York during the previous year, and the American title, *Prancing Nigger*, was substituted in later English editions for the original one—doubtless owing to the comparative success which the book had achieved in the States. The dropping of the original title is a matter for some regret: *Prancing Nigger* has a rather cheap, rumbustious quality ill-suited to any Firbank novel, and particularly to those of the later, " tragic " period. It was suggested in New York, as I have already mentioned, that *Prancing Nigger* should be turned into a " musical extravaganza," and had this project materialized, the American label might have served well enough; but *Sorrow in Sunlight* is surely the better title for the novel, and might well be revived for future reprints.

If *The Flower beneath the Foot* has come to represent, for English critics, the most typically " Firbankian " of the novels, *Prancing Nigger* was and is by far the most widely popular. In America it made Firbank's name, and even in England ran through several editions, being reprinted not only in the

" Rainbow " edition, but also in Messrs. Duckworth's " New Readers' Library " (in the company of Galsworthy, Blunden, Gorki, etc.). *Prancing Nigger* is, in fact, Firbank's nearest approach to a conventional " novel," and has a very good claim to be his best one. Considered as an æsthetic whole, I suppose it *is* his best: it has a very definite story, the design of the book is not obscured by over-decoration, the writing has a fluent ease which Firbank had never achieved before. *Prancing Nigger* succeeds, in fact, where *Inclinations* (and *Caprice*, too, to some extent) failed: the facility never lapses into silliness or into the exclamatory " Dadaism " of the earlier books; the prose is a perfect blend of the two " manners " represented by *Caprice* and *Valmouth*. To me, indeed, *Prancing Nigger* seems almost too perfect: and if I dispute its claim to be Firbank's best novel, it is precisely for this rather paradoxical reason. It may sound like an over-refinement of taste, but it seems to me that the best of Firbank is inseparable from his imperfections; one comes to admire him for his defects, they are perhaps the irritant grains of sand which produce the pearls. *Prancing Nigger*, for all its rather over-ripe perfection, seems to me never to rise quite to the level of his best work: there is no passage, I think, which is comparable to (for instance) the storm scene in *Valmouth*, or even to the Sapphic supper party in *Vainglory*.

I think, in fact, that *Prancing Nigger*, though an admirable novel, is not primarily a Firbank novel at all; it is, rather, a novel about negroes by Ronald Firbank. In it Firbank was attempting something he had not attempted before: he set out to write a book on a given subject, i.e. negroes; *Prancing Nigger*, in fact, is almost a *roman à thèse*. The attempt is successful: but it seems to me that the very best of Firbank is to be found in those works which are purely the product of his own phantasy. Not that *Prancing Nigger* can be called, by any stretch of imagination, a realistic novel; but Cuna-Cuna does bear a certain distant relationship to Haiti, and there may, one feels (and certainly one hopes), be somewhere in the world a negress like Mrs. Mouth (whereas Mrs. Yaj, of *Valmouth*, is, in the words of her creator, " figurable perhaps to nothing so much as something from below ").

I have said that *Prancing Nigger* is almost a *roman à thèse*, and no doubt it has already been classified, by American professors, under some recondite sub-category of the " negro novel." It is a far cry, certainly, from *Prancing Nigger* to *Uncle Tom's Cabin*; but in the story of the Mouth family one can, I suppose, if so minded, detect some faint adumbration of a " moral "—the corruption of peasant simplicity by urban sophistication. I am not suggesting for one moment that Firbank, in *Prancing Nigger*, had any such solemn intention; but of all his books it is the only one (apart from *Odette*) in which even the faintest *awareness* of moral issues is apparent. As it happens, vice triumphs over virtue, and Firbank betrays no prejudice here more than elsewhere against the corruptions of urbanity—rather the reverse. The " moral " of the story is enclosed, to so speak, in ironic inverted commas; yet its presence, however parenthetic, explains, I think, the fact that *Prancing Nigger* is Firbank's most popular novel and the easiest to read. Popular fiction is, after all, based (quite rightly) on the antithesis of good and evil. The trouble with highbrows is, as Mr. E. M. Forster says[1] of one of his characters, that they are chiefly aware not so much of " Good and Evil " as of " good-and-evil." Firbank, one feels, was happily unaware of both these aspects of duality.

Prancing Nigger is set, as we have seen, in a Caribbean

[1] In *The Longest Journey*.

island which has points in common with Haiti, and the story
is concerned with the adventures of a negro family, Mr. and
Mrs. Ahmadou Mouth and their children.   Mrs. Mouth
conceives the idea of a migration from Mediavilla, the
fishing village where they live, to Cuna-Cuna, the gay
island capital:

> " ' We leave Mediavilla for de education ob my daughters,' she
> would say. . . . ' We go to Cuna-Cuna for de finishing ob *mes filles* ' "

Her husband, happy with his hymn tunes and his Bible,
disapproves of the project:

> " ' How often hab I bid you nebba to mention dat modern Sodom
> in de hearing ob my presence ! ' "

He is overruled, however, and the family prepare for the
move—much to the distress of Miami, the eldest daughter,
who has lost her heart to a young fisherman, Bamboo.   Her
sister Edna, however, welcomes the change; so does their
little brother Charlie, who makes the journey to the town on
foot, for the purpose of collecting butterflies:

> " ' Have you nothing, young man, to declare ? '
> " ' . . . Butterfles ! '
> " ' Exempt of duty.   Pass ! ' . . . "

The Mouth family rent a " charming freehold villa " from
a Madame Ruiz (" a lady of influence and wealth—the widow
of the Inventor of Sunflower Piquant ").   Her son, a young
man of esoteric temperament, and a composer, " had been
from his earliest years the source of his mother's constant
chagrin and despair.   At the age of five he had assaulted his
nurse, and steadily onward his passions had grown and
grown. . . . "   Later: " His *Three Hodeidahs* and *Five Phallic
Dances for Pianoforte and Orchestra*, otherwise known as
' Suite in Green,' had taken the whole concert world by
storm. . . . "

This versatile personage is soon conducting a liaison with
Edna Mouth.   The rest of the family react to the charms of
Cuna-Cuna with varying degrees of enthusiasm:

" Leaning from a balcony of the Grand Savannah Hotel, their
instincts all aroused, Miami and Edna gazed out across the Alameda,
a place all foliage, lamplight and flowers.   It was the hour when
Society, in slowly parading carriages, would congregate to take the
air beneath the pale mimosas that adorned the favourite promenade.
All but recumbent, as though agreeably fatigued by their recent
emotions (what wild follies were not committed in shuttered villas
during the throbbing hours of noon?), the Cunans in their elegant
equipages, made . . . an interesting and absorbing sight." . . .

The Ciné Lara, the Café McDhu'l, the " Dancings " exert
their dangerous attractions. . . . Young Charlie Mouth, for
one, finds them irresistible:

" Passing before the Café de Cuna, and a people's ' Dancing,' he
roamed leisurely along. Incipient Cyprians, led by vigilant blanched-
faced queens, youths of a certain life, known as bwam-wam bwam-
wams, gaunt pariah dogs with questing eyes, all equally were on the
prowl. . . . Pursuing the glittering thoroughfare, it was interesting
to observe the pleasure announcements of the various theatres,
picked out in signs of fire: Aïda: The Jewels of the Madonna: Clara
Novotny and Lily Lima's Season." . . .

Mrs. Mouth's enthusiasm is tempered by the fact that Nini
Snagge, an old family friend who has preceded her to the
town, is now an inmate of a " house of ill-fame."   Mr. Mouth
is virtuously indignant:

" ' Understand dat any sort ob intimacy 'tween de villa an' de
Closerie des Lilas Ah must flatly forbid.'
" ' Prancing Nigger, as ef I should take your innocent chillens to
call on po' Nini; not dat eberyt'ing about her at de Closerie is not
elegant and nice. Sh'o, some ob de inmates ob dat establishment
possess mo' diamonds dan dair betters do outside! ' "

But Mr. Mouth takes a poor view, on the whole, of urban
pleasures:

" 'Ah set out to look fo' de Meetin'-House, but no sooner am Ah in de street dan a female wid her har droopin' loose down ober her back an' into her eyes, she tell me to come along!'

" ' Some of dose bold women, dey ought to be shot through dair bottoms!' Mrs. Mouth indignantly said. . . . "

Miami, unlike her sister and brother, remains uncorrupted by the city's glamour, and faithful to her fisherman-lover, Bamboo. The Mouths go into society, there is an earthquake and a religious revival; but the family begin to tire at last of urban splendours; Mrs. Mouth is outraged by the snobism of Cunan society; news comes at last of the death of Bamboo in the earthquake. . . . The book closes with a penitential procession, in which the heart-broken Miami takes part: observed unsympathetically from a window by her sister Edna and her protector:

" ' Perspirin', an' her skirt draggin', sh'o, she looked a fright.'

" He smiled: for indeed already the world was perceptibly moulding her. . . .

" ' Oh honey! . . . Dair's a new dancer at de Apollo to-night; suppose we go?' . . . "

Prancing Nigger is really a story of sacred and profane love—with profane love triumphing in the end. Here again, too, as in *The Flower beneath the Foot*, we can detect in the quasi-" tragic " *dénouement* a reference to Firbank's own frustrations: once more romance is nipped in the bud—this time by an earthquake. It is evident, too, I think, that in Charlie Mouth, eternally in quest of his " butterflies," Firbank is for once employing a conscious symbolism. (Compare Niri-Esther, at the end of *Valmouth*, " waywardly in pursuit of—a butter-fly.") Charlie sees Cuna-Cuna at first entirely in terms of butterflies:

" So many sparkling fans. One, a delicate mauve one: ' Shucks! If only you wa' butterflies!' he breathed, contemplating with avidity the nonchalant throng; then perceiving a richer specimen splashed with silver of the same amative tint: ' Oh you lil beauty! ' And, clutching his itching net to his heart, he regretfully withdrew. . . . "

Later, more sophisticated, he frequents the bars and the bwam-wam bwam-wams (whose " equivocal behaviour," during the earthquake, was " perhaps more shocking even than the shocks "); after the " quake," however, he seems to become, temporarily at least, a reformed character:

> " ' I mizzable sinner, Lord. You heah, Sah? You heah me say dat? Oh, Jesus, Jesus, Jesus,' and weeping, he threw himself down among a bed of flowers. . . . Above him, great spikes of blossom were stirring in the idle wind, while birds were chaunting volun-taries among the palms. And in thanksgiving, too, arose the matin bells. From Our Lady of the Pillar, from the Church of La Favavoa in the West . . . " etc.

Here, once again, we detect an echo of *Odette* and *Santal*: " idle wind," " chaunting voluntaries," the names of churches, etc. Like Laura de Nazianzi, like Cherif in *Santal*, Charlie Mouth seeks solace in religion; and so, perhaps, might Firbank have done, if things had been just a little different, if it weren't, after all, rather a bore. . . . " The Church wouldn't have me, so I mock at her ": one wonders what tragedy lay concealed beneath that evasive remark made to Lord Berners.

Yes—*Prancing Nigger* is a long way after *Uncle Tom's Cabin;* none the less, Firbank's negroes are his nearest approach to " realism." The white characters in *Prancing Nigger* are pure Firbank; the negroes, however, are something more—or less, whichever one cares to think. It is interesting to speculate whether Firbank, had he lived, would have developed this aspect of his talent; the signs, such as they are, seem to point in the contrary direction, for his next work is a reversion to an earlier mode.

(III)

Concerning the Eccentricities of Cardinal Pirelli, Firbank's last novel, appeared after his death in 1926; the original edition contains a portrait by Augustus John.

Pirelli has acquired, in certain circles, a notoriety independent of its æsthetic merits: it is Firbank's most indecorous novel, and had it attracted wider notice at the time of its publication, might well have come under the censor's ban. As it was, *Pirelli*, like all Firbank's books, made an unobtrusive entry into the world, and its reputation was (and I suppose still is) confined to a limited public.

One guesses that in this, his last book, Firbank's emotional frustration, exacerbated by his failing health and by his apprehension of an early death, reached boiling point; topics which, in his previous work, he had merely hinted at, are here treated without disguise; *Cardinal Pirelli* is, so to speak, Firbank's final fling, a gesture of defiance directed at the smug middle-class morality which he despised.

Monsignor Parr (in *Vainglory*) was, it may be remembered, " temperamental, when not otherwise . . . employed." The same might be said of Cardinal Pirelli, but in his case those " other " employments, far from being tactfully concealed by a row of dots, are revealed with an unblushing particularity.

The style of *Pirelli* is in complete contrast with that of *Prancing Nigger;* Firbank has here reverted to the manner of *Valmouth:* " plot " is once more subordinated to a series of elaborate " set-pieces," the texture of the prose is dense and overloaded, the characters crowd about the central figure in an atmosphere heavy with incense and innuendo. The setting is Spain—but not, one feels. (although the references are contemporary), the Spain of the twentieth century. The book exhales all the splendour and corruption of the late Renaissance; the Cardinal himself, despite his up-to-date accoutrements, is a figure straight out of the *seicento*. (It is surprising, by the way, that *Pirelli* should be the first of Firbank's novels to have a Spanish background, for the country had exercised upon him, from his earliest days, a powerful fascination. One can only assume that he postponed his Spanish novel until such time as he felt capable of doing it the fullest justice. It is worth noting that *Valmouth*, the nearest of the earlier works to *Pirelli* in point of style, is full of Spanish references, and has, indeed, in spite of the quasi-English setting, a perceptibly " Spanish " atmosphere.)

Pirelli has no " plot " and, indeed, very little story at all: an alternative title might be " Scenes from the Life of Cardinal Pirelli." Once again the theme is " tragic "; but the protagonist, on this occasion, has little in common, superficially, with Laura de Nazianzi or with Charlie Mouth. His tragedy is hardly a tragedy of innocence: no one, surely, could be less like Odette than Don Alvaro Narciso Hernando Pirelli, Cardinal-Archbishop of Clemenza. . . . And yet, oddly enough, one does perceive a parallel between the downfall of the Cardinal and the theme of all Firbank's later novels. It may be a far cry from Charlie Mouth to Don Alvaro: but the Cardinal, too, is in his own manner a chaser of " butterflies "—those ephemeral and elusive charmers which, once captured, prove always a disappointment, wilting and fading in the hand which seizes them. . . . *Cardinal Pirelli* is at once a tragedy of lost youth and of the pagan temperament caught in the toils of contemporary " Christian " civilization. Like Monsignor Parr, Don Alvaro is himself " something between a butterfly and a misanthrope "; and his final agonized swoopings upon Chicklet, the choirboy, are not, after all, so very far removed from Charlie Mouth's ecstatic pursuit of those " azure soledads, and radiant conquistadors " in the savannah. Himself approaching middle-age, and already under the shadow of death, Firbank put more than a little of his own frustration, his sense of the *lacrimæ rerum* into the character of the Cardinal—just as he had identified himself, to a large extent, with Laura de Nazianzi and Miami Mouth. *Cardinal Pirelli* is, paradoxically enough, not only one of Firbank's funniest novels, but also one of his most serious.

Don Alvaro, Cardinal-Archbishop of Clemenza (" in white Andalucia "), is far from being an orthodox prelate. The novel opens with the account of a grandiose ceremony in the Cathedral—" a christening—and not a child's ":

> " Monsignor Silex moved a finger from forehead to chin, and from ear to ear. The Duquesa Dun Eden's escapades, if continued, would certainly cost the Cardinal his hat. . . . Monsignor Silex crossed his breast. He must gather force to look about him. Frame a close report. The Pontiff, in far-off Italy, would expect precision. . . . "

The recipient, in fact, of this unorthodox baptism is none other than the Duquesa Dun Eden's " week-old police-dog ":

> " ' Mother's pet! ' she cooed, as the imperious creature passed his tongue across the splendid uncertainty of her chin. . . . ' No, my naughty blessing; no, not now! . . . By and by, a *bone*.'
>
> " Words which brought the warm saliva to the expectant parent's mouth.
>
> " Tail awag, sex apparent (to the affected slight confusion of the Infanta Eulalia-Irene), he crouched, his eyes fixed wistfully upon the nozzle of his son. . . .
>
> " But, supported by the Prior of the Cartuja, the Cardinal had arisen for the act of Immersion.
>
> " Of unusual elegance, with the remains, moreover, of perfect looks, he was as wooed and run after by the ladies as any matador.
>
> " ' And thus being cleansed and purified, I do call thee " Crack," ' he addressed the Duquesa's captive burden." . . .

But the christening of police-dogs is only one of a number of unorthodox practices which, reaching by indirect means the Pontiff's ears, will contribute at last to the Cardinal's downfall. Nor do the details of his private life (duly transmitted by Phoebe Poco, his housekeeper) find favour with the authorities; he is too often tempted to indulge in " what prurient persons might term, perhaps, a ' frolic ' "—in other words, to " forsake the Palace for the Plaza ":

" The dear street. The adorable Avenidas. The quickening stimulus of the throng. . . . Disguised as a caballero from the provinces or as a matron (disliking to forgo altogether the militant bravoura of a skirt), it became possible to combine philosophy, equally, with pleasure. . . . And how entrancing to perch on a barstool, over a glass of old golden sherry!

"Although a mortification, it was imperative to bear in mind the consequences of cutting a too-dashing figure. Beware display. Vanity once had proved all but fatal: ' I remember it was the night I wore ringlets and was called " my queen " ' " . . .

Indeed, were it not for " paternostering Phoebe Poco " he might be tempted to forget altogether the cares of his diocese:

" 'Ah, Don Alvaro, sir! Come here . . . Don Alvaro, there is mischief in the air! '

" ' Mischief? '

" ' In certain quarters of the city you would take it almost for some sortilege! '

" ' What next? '

" 'At the *Encarnacion* there's nothing, of late, but seediness. Sister Engracia with the chicken-pox, and Mother Claridad with the itch, while at the College of Noble Damosels, in the Calle Santa Fé, I hear a daughter of Don José Illescas, in a fit of caprice, has set a match to her coronet.'

" 'A match to her what? ' . . . "

As in *Vainglory* and *Valmouth*, the " story " threads its way leisurely through a series of carefully built-up scenes, thronged with characters, most of them merely glimpsed in passing: Marvilla de las Espinafres (" airing anti-patriotic views on birth-control. . . . ' Certainly not; most decidedly *no*! I should scream!' "); the Duquesa Dun Eden, with her penchant for police-dogs; the philoprogenitive Marchioness of las Cubas (" they say she jobs her mules "); negresses, choir-boys, English governesses, etc. (" Clemenza," indeed, though nominally Spanish, suggests some not-so-remote colony of Pisuerga.)

The whispering-campaign against the Cardinal is skilfully built up:

" ' He is delicious in handsomeness tonight!'

" 'A shade battered. But a lover's none the worse in my opinion for acquiring technique.' . . .

" 'A lover! What? His Eminence . . .? '

" The Duchess tittered.

" ' Why not? I expect he has a little woman to whom he takes off his clothes,' she murmured, turning to admire the wondrous *Madonna of the Mule-Mill* attributed to Murillo. . . . "

Note, by the way, how after a more than usually devastating remark, Firbank skids adroitly aside into some elaborate fragment of description, e.g. " . . . she murmured, turning to admire the wondrous *Madonna*," etc. It is one of Firbank's favourite tricks, and becomes increasingly frequent in the later novels. Often he uses it with great skill, as in the above-quoted passage, where one's attention is instantly diverted from the Cardinal's amours to the picture above the speaker's head. The effect is to " soft-pedal " the gossip about Pirelli into a banal matter-of-factness, thereby vastly enhancing its effect. The juxtaposition, moreover, of the Cardinal's " little woman" with the " *Madonna of the Mule-Mill*," apparently accidental, is a masterly touch.

Not the least successful chapter in the book is that describing the discussions, at the Vatican, of the " scandals of Clemenza ":

" Saluting the sovereign Pontiff with deep obeisance, the Cardinal came directly to the point.

" ' These schisms in Spain.' . . .

" ' They are ever before me,' His Holiness confessed.

" ' With priests like Pirelli, the Church is in peril! ' "

The Pope (in person) has made few incursions into English fiction—Baron Corvo's Hadrian VII is the only other example which springs immediately to mind. Tertius II, in *Pirelli*, wears his tiara lightly enough:

" He had the head of an elderly lady's maid, and an expression concealed by layers of tactful caution.

" ' Why can't they all behave? ' he asked himself, plaintively.' . . . "

His Holiness, for his part, is rather bored by the " schisms in Spain," but the Cardinal is insistent:

" ' If I may tender the advice of the secret Consistory,' he said, ' Your Holiness should Listen-in.'

" ' To what end? '

" 'A snarl, a growl, a bark, a yelp, coming from the font, would be quite enough to condemn.' . . .

" ' Per Bacco—I should take it for a baby.'

" ' . . . condemn . . . this Pirelli for a *maleficus pastor*. In which case, the earlier, the better, the unfrocking.' . . . "

Whether His Holiness listens-in or not we are not told. But Cardinal Pirelli, getting wind of the campaign against him, " flees the capital," and retires to an abandoned monastery in the mountains, there to meditate upon the Church's sad decline:

" The forsaken splendour of the vast closed cloisters seemed almost to augur the waning of a cult. Likewise the decline of Apollo, Diana, Isis, with the gradual downfall of their temples, had been heralded, in past times, by the dispersal of their priests. It looked as though Mother Church, like Venus or Diana, was making way in due turn for the beliefs that should follow: ' and we shall begin again with intolerance, martyrdom and converts,' the Cardinal ruminated, pausing before an ancient fresco depicting the eleven thousand virgins, or as many as there was room for. . . . "

This seems to me the most surprising passage in the whole of Firbank. Quite apart from its prophetic truth (though

Firbank may perhaps have "cribbed" this part of it), the passage is nearer to being completely serious than anything he ever wrote. It might almost be a quotation from Sir James Frazer—and in all likelihood Firbank had been dipping into *The Golden Bough*. Whatever its source, it is an astonishing interpolation. Firbank himself, one feels, must have found it slightly *gênant*, for he is careful to conclude the passage with one of his little "skids" into humorous incongruity (the "eleven thousand virgins," etc.).

One can detect, in these last chapters of *Pirelli*, a curious process in operation, a kind of splitting apart of Firbank's literary personality. It is as if two opposed elements in his style—the ninetyish sensibility and the cynical bawdiness—which up till now have been contrapuntally blended, had here diverged into disparate though still parallel channels. "Serious" passages alternate with riotously funny ones; and the two streams, once separated, seem to develop a new impetus: on the one hand a lushiness of sentiment, on the other an extremity of bawdiness such as Firbank has never before allowed himself. The novel closes with the Cardinal's satyr-like pursuit of Chicklet, the choirboy, through the darkened aisles of the Basilica—a "sarabandish and semi-mythic" Dance of Death, at the close of which Don Alvaro, "nude and elementary now as Adam himself," and with his object still unattained, falls lifeless before "a painting of old Dominic Theotocópuli, the Greek, showing the splendour of Christ's Martyrdom," where, in due course, he is discovered by Phoebe Poco:

> "Confused not a little at the sight before her, her equilibrium was only maintained by the recollection of her status: 'I'm an honest widow; so I know what men are, bless them! . . . So.' She stopped to coil her brier-wood chaplet about him in order that he might be less uncovered. 'It's wonderful what us bits of women do with a

string of beads, but they don't go far with a gentleman. . . . *Adios, Don Alvaro of my heart*,' she sighed, turning away towards the little garden door ajar.

" Through the triple windows of the chancel the sky was clear and blue—a blue like the blue of lupins. Above him stirred the wind-blown banners in the nave."

So ends the last chapter of Firbank's last novel—on a note which echoes his first published work, *Odette d'Antrevernes*. To my mind, this final chapter rather detracts from the novel as a whole, some passages of which are as good as anything Firbank ever achieved. The typically ninetyish combination of sanctity and smut was always a temptation to Firbank, and in his earlier works, where the fun predominates over the sentiment, he uses the mode effectively; here, however, he is too near to his ninetyish models, and the last chapter of *Pirelli* has something of the repellent and rather embarrassing quality of *The Priest and the Acolyte*.

(IV)

I have shown how, in Firbank's last book, the two tendencies in his style diverge into two contrasted elements. I hope, also, that in the foregoing survey of his work, I have made clear that it is the blending of these two elements—the *fin-de-siècle* sensibility and the cynical self-mockery—which gives his style its particular flavour. It is interesting to speculate whether, in different circumstances, Firbank might have written differently. Living when he did, he could not, I think, have developed otherwise; it is possible, however, that had he been born twenty years earlier, had he, that is to say, been an adult instead of a schoolboy during the Mauve Epoch, he might have avoided the dichotomy in his personality, and instead of mocking at his own pretensions, have contrived to take himself, as a writer, *au grand sérieux*. He might, in other words, have continued to write in the style of *Odette d'Antrevernes*. Had he done so, he would, there is no doubt, have developed into a competent enough writer of a kind; the ninetyish passages in *Pirelli*, if not very remarkable, are at least a great technical improvement on *Odette*. But it is safe to say that, had he not learned to laugh at himself, he would have remained a rather undistinguished minor writer, and would by this time have been long forgotten.

A man of the nineties born out of his time, he made the only sort of adaptation of which he was capable; despite his *fin-de-sièclisme*, we think of him—if he must be assigned to a period—as typical of the nineteen-twenties. So, indeed, he was: but he was also something more. Any writer who is to survive must possess to some degree the quality of timelessness: we do not think of *Pride and Prejudice*, for instance, or *Alice in Wonderland* or *The Importance of being Earnest* as products of any particular period. Firbank, I think, belongs to the same timeless category: he is nothing so boring as a " great " writer, or even one who " has to be read "; he is not " important "; on the other hand he will never, I believe, be quite forgotten: one will continue, now and again, to come across *Valmouth* or *Vainglory* on the special shelf which people keep for those books which they read purely for pleasure. It may not be a very distinguished fate for an author; but it is one with which Ronald himself would, I think, have been perfectly satisfied.

BIBLIOGRAPHY

Odette d'Antrevernes and *A Study in Temperament*. Elkin Mathews, 1905.

Vainglory. With a Frontispiece by Félicien Rops. Grant Richards, 1915.

Odette. With four illustrations and cover-design by Albert Buhrer. Grant Richards, 1916.

Inclinations. With two drawings by Albert Rutherston. Grant Richards, 1916.

Caprice. With a Frontispiece by Augustus John. Grant Richards, 1917.

Valmouth: A Romantic Novel. With a Frontispiece by Augustus John. Grant Richards, 1919.

The Princess Zoubaroff: A Comedy. With a Frontispiece and decorations by Michel Sevier. Grant Richards, 1920.

Santal. Grant Richards, 1921.

The Flower beneath the Foot. With a decoration by C. R. W. Nevinson and portraits by Augustus John and Wyndham Lewis. Grant Richards, 1923.

Prancing Nigger. With an Introduction by Carl van Vechten and a Frontispiece by R. E. Locher. New York, Brentano's, 1924.

Sorrow in Sunlight (*Prancing Nigger*). With end-papers by C. R. W. Nevinson. Brentano's (London), 1925.

Concerning the Eccentricities of Cardinal Pirelli. With a portrait by Augustus John. Grant Richards, 1926.

The Collected Works of Ronald Firbank. With an Introduction by Arthur Waley and an essay by Osbert Sitwell. Duckworth, 1929.

The Artificial Princess. With an Introduction by Sir Coleridge Kennard. Duckworth, 1934.

Five Novels. By Ronald Firbank. (*Valmouth, Prancing Nigger, The Flower beneath the Foot, The Artificial Princess, Concerning the Eccentricities of Cardinal Pirelli.*) With an Introduction by Sir Osbert Sitwell and a portrait by Augustus John. Duckworth, 1949.

The following were reprinted by Messrs. Duckworth in the uniform "Rainbow" edition (1929–30):

Prancing Nigger.
Valmouth.
The Flower beneath the Foot.
Concerning the Eccentricities of Cardinal Pirelli.
Caprice.
Inclinations.
Vainglory.
The Princess Zoubaroff.

Prancing Nigger was also issued by Messrs. Duckworth in the "New Reader's Library" in 1931.

Page references in this book are to the "Rainbow" edition, except where otherwise stated.

Books and Other Writings dealing with Ronald Firbank

CONNOLLY, CYRIL: *The Condemned Playground: Essays 1927–1944.* Routledge, 1945.

—— : *Enemies of Promise.* Routledge, 1938.

DICKINSON, PATRIC: *A Note on Ronald Firbank* (1886–1915–1926). Contributed to *The Windmill* (edited by Reginald Moore and Edward Lane). Heinemann, 1946.

FORSTER, E. M.: *Ronald Firbank* (Essay), *Abinger Harvest.* Arnold, 1936.

KYRLE FLETCHER, I: *Ronald Firbank: a Memoir;* with personal reminiscences by Lord Berners, V. B. Holland, Augustus John, R.A., and Osbert Sitwell. Portraits by Alvaro Guevara, Augustus John, R.A., Wyndham Lewis and Charles Shannon, R.A. Duckworth, 1930.

SITWELL OSBERT: *Ronald Firbank;* an essay printed in Firbank's *Collected Works,* Duckworth, 1929. (This is the same as that included in Ifan Kyrle Fletcher's *Memoir.*)

WALEY, ARTHUR: *Introduction* to Firbank's *Collected Works.* Duckworth, 1929.

WAUGH, EVELYN: *Ronald Firbank:* an essay contributed to *Life and Letters,* Vol. II, No. 10 (1929).

INDEX